.comPREHENSIVE

www.dotcomprehensive.com

I0011612

A Step-by-Step Guide to
Bring Your Business Online

A Road Map to Successful

Site Creation

James **M** Helmering

Copyright © 2014 James Helmering
All rights reserved.
ISBN-13: 978-0615998787
ISBN-10: 061599878X

IMPORTANT COPYRIGHT AND LEGAL NOTICE:

This publication is protected under the US Copyright Act of 1976 and all other applicable international, federal, state, and local laws and all rights are reserved, including resale rights: you are not allowed to give or sell this guide to anyone else. If you feel you've received a pirated and/or stolen copy, please contact us via e-mail at legal@dotcomprehensive.com and notify us of the situation.

Please note that much of this publication is based on personal experience and anecdotal evidence. Although the author and publisher have made every reasonable attempt to achieve complete accuracy of the content in this guide, they assume no responsibility for errors or omissions. Also, you should use this information as you see fit, and at your own risk. Your particular situation may not be exactly suited to the examples illustrated here; in fact, it's likely that they won't be the same, and you should adjust your use of the information and recommendations accordingly.

Any trademarks, service marks, product names or named features are assumed to be the property of their respective owners, and are used only for reference. There is no implied endorsement if we use one of these terms.

Some of the details have been modified to protect the author and all other parties involved.

Finally, use your head. Nothing in this guide is intended to replace common sense, legal, or other professional advice, and is meant to inform and entertain the reader.

Contents

<u>Acknowledgements</u>

I would like to thank everyone involved in making this book a reality. The amount of time it takes to create a book that backs the keyword in this book's title "comprehensive" but maintains simplicity for the reader is a challenging assignment.

First, I would like to thank Tera Huesgen and Megan Peters for their editorial achievements and attention to detail. Their contribution to this guide ensures that the readers attain quality information. Without their involvement, this book would not have been possible.

I would also like to thank my cousin Bethany Kellogg for assisting me with the book's cover art and design. Bethany also provided her astonishing marketing perspective that greatly helped the success of this book.

Many thanks to my uncle, Bob Kellogg, for adding his input and expertise within various pages of the book.

Most importantly, I want to thank my mother, Melanie Donovan, for allowing me to use her home as an office while I completed my goals and followed my dreams.

Finally, a special thanks to everyone who doubted the completion of this book. Your negative support was the inspiration I needed to complete it.

Dear readers,

A couple of things need to be discussed before you begin reading.

1.) Sometimes different browsers cause particular services (taught in this book) to function incorrectly or not work at all. As frustrating as it may seem, there is a simple solution to this issue. At the end of the **Introduction** (starting on the next page) you will install several browsers onto your computer. These browsers are used for testing your site, which will be discussed later in the book. It is also recommended to use a different browser if you are having issues with a particular section in this book due to improper functionality.

2.) The Internet is constantly evolving. All screen shots and demonstrations were up-to-date at the time of this book's creation but may have changed depending on the date of your purchase.

Please accept and understand that this book is merely a guide and some screen shots and/or steps provided may not be EXACTLY to date but the process will likely be the same.

Introduction

There are hundreds, perhaps even thousands of books online today that supposedly teach individuals how to get their very own WordPress site up and running in just a few short days with very little difficulty. I have personally read some of these books and found that even with the five-plus years of online experience that I have accumulated, including some developing background, they were far from understandable.

Most of these so-called programs/books assume that the people using them have the knowledge to do some tasks that I still find difficult at times.

I first started my online venture when I was 18 years old. My only prior experience with a computer was using Microsoft office. The only reason I had this knowledge was because it was mandatory for the majority of my school projects and book reports.

When I first dipped my feet into the world of online businesses, I literally did not know the first thing about a website other than visiting them for information. In fact, it took me months of reading "over my head" articles and playing with various site builders before I was able to create a simple blog.

Even WordPress was difficult to use because I had never used it before and all of the articles I read were written by people who had plenty of experience building them but lacked the effort to thoroughly explain how they did it. Nothing was explained in a way that could help people get a site up and running with little effort.

Today, I am very experienced and I know there are those who wish to have the skills to build a site of their own, but have no clue where to start.

In this book, I am going take you by the hand and show you step-by-step what to do from purchasing a domain right down to hosting it and putting up a website that you proudly created.

I will take you through an entire step-by-step process that I wish I had available to me when I was first starting out online. If you were getting ready to take a test on site creation that allowed you to use one resource and you chose this book, prepare to get an A!

This book is very detailed. Some sections will be much easier than others but as long as you follow along, it will be difficult to NOT complete each task. Everything here is explained in a way that is easy to comprehend, yet suitable for everyone.

At times, you may find yourself asking why a section is interpreted so thoroughly. You may even find it to be pretentious, but please understand it is for the greater good.

A section that may seem simple to you might be complicated for others who have no experience. The important matter is that they took that leap of faith and brought their desire to learn with them on their journey.

At the end of each section a set of tasks will be presented and should be completed before moving any further. Skipping ahead just to be further along in the book will only create more work for you. Finish this entire book and complete each task and I promise that you will have your very own website proudly making a mark in online real estate.

Some of the services we talk about in this book require a fee such as purchasing a domain, and buying a host to home your domain. I did not write this book to recommend services with which I am affiliated. I wrote this book to show you how to get a professional website, online, by yourself.

I could teach you how to host your site for free, but remember, you get what you pay for and that is especially true in the online world.

Please refer to the table of contents at any time for a detailed list of topics taught in this guide. If throughout this course you have any questions, please email our support team at: support@dotcomprehensive.com.

It's time to get started. As I stated earlier, you will have action steps to complete before you move to another section.

Action Steps

1.) Install Different Web Browsers For Testing

It's time to familiarize you with a few more browsers. You will need different browsers in the future for testing purposes because your site may function properly on one and not another.

Download Safari (PC Users), Firefox, and Google Chrome.

Internet Explorer is not available to Mac users. If you are using a PC you already have Internet Explorer installed by default.

support.apple.com/downloads/#safari

http://firefox.com

http://google.com/chrome

Section 1
Domain Names

What is a Domain Name?

Most of you already know what a domain name is, and some of you may already have a few that have been sitting around collecting virtual dust because you have no idea how to give them a home.

A domain name is an identification string that defines a realm of administrative autonomy, authority, or control on the Internet (wikipedia.org, 2014).

It is a memorable address that is owned by you and used by others for accessing a website to which you point.

This section will help you understand the purpose of a domain and teach you how to purchase one that suits your site.

Your domain name will be unique to your site and based on what you sell. It is advisable to have a domain name that relates to what you are selling, with the exception of product branding.

Branding a product can be difficult for someone with no prior web or marketing skills. Although, it is actually beneficial in the end because people make purchases based on brands they know and trust.

A good example of a successful brand name that isn't related to the products they sell would be a company called Apple. Although an apple has nothing to do with a computer it is one of the first things that come to mind when hearing the term.

Before you get too excited about domain ownership, you will need to create an account with GoDaddy so you can begin the arduous journey of domain hunting.

Signing Up to GoDaddy.com

Though there are other services online that allow you to purchase domain names, GoDaddy's reputation is rather superior when compared. Their sign up process is exceptionally easier than their competitors, thus saving you time and that is what this book is trying to teach you.

We're not going to waste any time. Type GoDaddy.com in your Internet browser's address bar and register a new account.

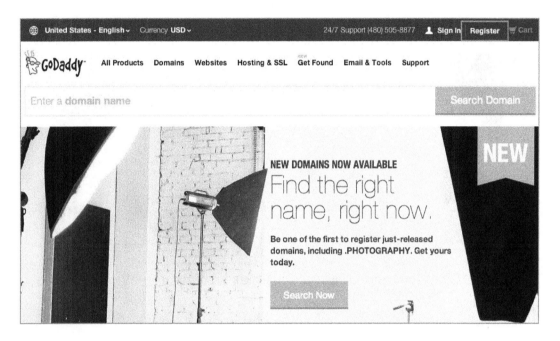

Next locate **New Customer** and click **Create My Account**. This will bring up an easy sign-up form for new memberships.

After filling out the form you will be asked to verify your email address. Once verified, your account becomes active granting you full access. Return to the home page by clicking the **GoDaddy** logo.

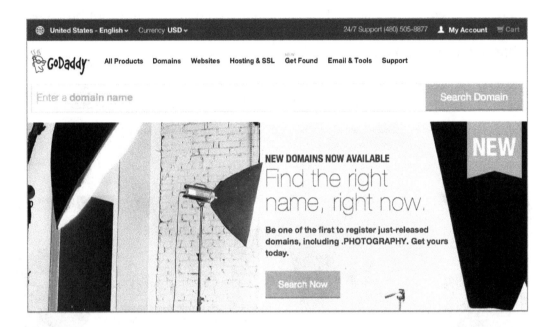

Feel free to take a moment and familiarize yourself with this site by clicking through the links. Or you may search for various domain names and acquire firsthand domain hunting experience. Finding a good domain name that hasn't been taken is very difficult, which is why it can be a tedious task.

Once you have had your fun exploring GoDaddy and are familiar with the functionality of the site, you can prepare yourself for the next lesson on proper domain searching.

Finding available domains can be frustrating and time consuming, but the good news is it can bring out the creativity that you might have lost years ago.

Action Step

Sign Up to GoDaddy.com

1.) Go to GoDaddy.com and create a new membership by following the instructions in this section.

Section 1.2
Domain Names

Finding an Adequate Domain Name

Finding a domain that meets the criteria of your site is difficult these days.

Some companies acquire numerous domain names with the intent of selling them at a higher price. Domains can be reasonably purchased for around eight dollars, but every domain has a price that someone might be willing to pay.

When a quality domain is available, the company will purchase it and become the proud owner of a domain name that someone else may be willing to buy for thousands of dollars.

Once a domain is purchased the company sticks a "For Sale" sign on it with an outrageous price that most find unreasonable. The majority of these domains won't sell right away, but when a sale is made the company comes out ahead.

This doesn't mean you should get discouraged. It's still very easy to obtain a desirable name. You just need two things: Your mind and your creativity.

Writing Down Benefits to Formulate A Name

Before I start the intricate hunt for a domain name, I write down all of the benefits of my product on a piece of paper. Within my product's benefits, I will highlight specific words that I find fun and enticing. Those highlighted words go into a list to form a large directory of potential names for my site.

Once my list is complete, I can take chosen words and put them together with other words to come up with a combination for an equally respectable domain name.

It's doubtful that you will find an available domain name with two words put together, correctly spelled and highly unlikely to find a name that consists of one correctly spelled word. But it never hurts to search GoDaddy and see for yourself.

No one knows your product like you do. So, right now, I want you to get out a piece of paper and write down all the benefits of your product. Don't stop! Write until you have written your product out of a job.

Highlight keywords within the list of benefits that are relevant and suitable for your product. Put your highlighted words together with other words, mix them up, and just have fun with this creative process.

Formulate an exorbitant amount of names so you can later make a firm decision on one that sticks. Each name you craft should be written down and forgotten while the next is being crafted. Until the list of names engulfs the paper you're writing on, do not stop creating. Your ideas will grow with your list and when it's time to choose a name, you will be satisfied with your decision.

 STOP!

Don't get too far ahead of yourself. Put this book down for a day and begin formulating a list of domain names using the principles taught in this lesson.

Why a Strong List of Domains is Important

The reason I wanted you to work exceptionally hard on your list is so that you wouldn't make the same mistake I used to make.

I would come up with a name, buy it, and hate it five minutes later. Sure, domains are cheap, but blindly purchasing the first thing I thought of became expensive.

I did this every time I was at this stage and the outcome was a redundantly large credit card bill. Only one of the domains I bought was used for the website and you can bet money it was always the last one purchased. The rest were abandoned and left for expiration.

Hopefully, I've convinced you to make a mindful decision when it comes to making a domain purchase. Trust me, that first awesome name you came up with will still be there when you make your final decision.

The Good, The Bad, and The Ugly

You should have formulated a giant list of potential candidates for your website. Unfortunately, it's not over yet. Now I want you to write down the pros and cons of each name on your list. You can't lie to anyone other than yourself; so if you don't like a name, just throw it out. If you don't do it now, you will end up doing it later after you've already paid for it.

When you are finished, tally up the results. If it has more cons than pros, throw it out.

The names with more pros than cons get put aside until you have eliminated the duds.

Finally, number the winning names in order of preference.

Don't get too far ahead of yourself. Put this book down and eliminate the

domains that will not suffice.

Searching for Available Domain Names

It was a lot of work, but worth it, I promise. If you followed the previous lesson correctly, you won't have any regrets. The lesson was drawn out to ensure that you understand the importance of buying once, with no remorse.

Open up GoDaddy.com and bring your numbered list of domains to the table. If you haven't already, sign in to your account so you can purchase a name as soon as you find one available from your list. Begin the search starting on your favorite domain from your numbered list.

The process of finding my domain for this book and website wasn't any different than what I have had you do. I always practice what I teach, which is how I came up with the suitable name **dotcomPREHENSIVE**.

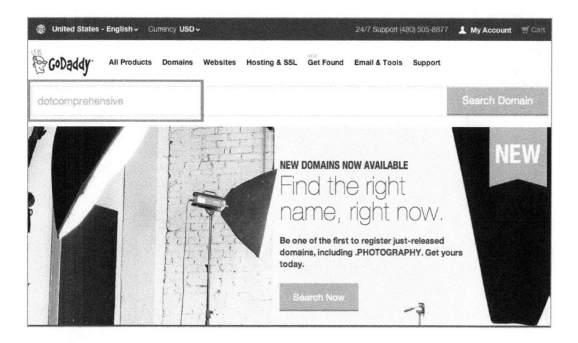

Purchasing Domains at A Discount

When you go down your list of potential domains, start from your favorite and work down the line. You will eventually hit the page, similar to the image below, letting you know it is available to purchase. Begin the checkout process but stay close to this book to avoid any unnecessary additional fees.

After clicking **Continue to Cart** you will be given three options: **Privacy**, **Options**, and **Email**. **Privacy** is optional if you wish to keep your domain's ownership and contact details private, for an additional fee, from the whois.com network.

We will not need **Options** or **Email** (located below **Privacy**) since we will be using other services for this domain so click **Continue to Cart**.

Let's review the current order. Wow, $73.85 seems a bit steep doesn't it? Select 1 year from the drop down menu and the price will be more reasonable.

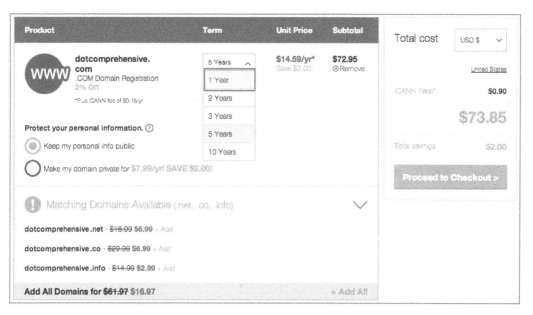

If you want a longer commitment, the choice is yours. I personally like to test my site's growth and profit for a year before committing to it any longer.

GoDaddy's clever scheme urges people to proceed to checkout without a discount. Luckily, you have this cheat sheet to help you avoid these operations.

Scroll to the bottom of the page and find the secluded promo venue. Keep this window active and open a new tab within your browser by pressing **Ctrl+T** for windows users or **Command+T** for Mac users.

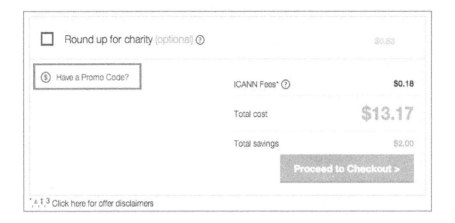

Go to Google and type in GoDaddy.com coupon codes.

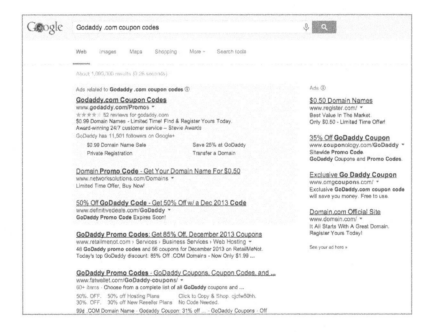

This task, although tedious, is worth the effort and can save you a lot of money down the road. Search by clicking through the various results presented to you, as each site will have multiple codes you can try.

Luckily, I found an active promo code on the first link at the top of Google's search results. You may or may not be as fortunate. Just remember, persistence is the key here.

As you can see on the image above, I managed to save $13.00. This was a special holiday promotion and finding such a deal is not always feasible. However, I wish the best of luck to you and your search.

Some extensive research may be required to find an active promo code. When one is found, copy it by pressing **Ctrl+C** for Windows users or **Command+C** for Mac users and paste it to the coupon box by pressing **Ctrl+V** for Windows users or **Command+V** for Mac users.

After applying the coupon to your order click **Proceed to Checkout**. Next you will need to select your payment method and fill out your billing information, which I have already done. Once completed click any of the buttons labeled **Place Your Order**.

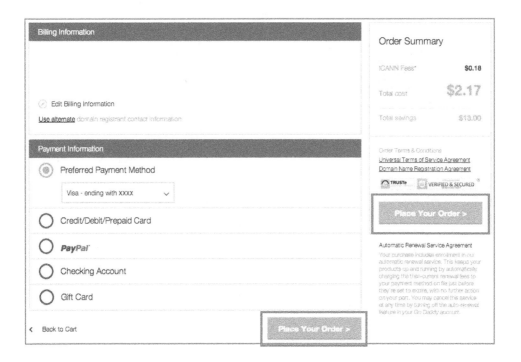

Congratulations! You are now the owner of a brand new, well-formulated domain name. But it's just a name and there is still a lot of work to be done in order to turn it into something of which you can be proud.

Action Steps

1.) Address Your Product's Benefits

List your product's benefits on a piece of paper. If you can't think of any, then maybe it's not worthy enough to promote.

2.) Highlight Relevant Keywords

Highlight all words within the benefits that are relevant, enticing, and fun. This will form a list of words you can use for crafting your domain.

3.) Craft Creative Domain Names

Take your list and start crafting potential domain names. Mix match, scramble, and/or play on other words until you have formed a large list.

4.) Eliminate the Unacceptable Names

Write the pros and cons of each name. If there are more cons than pros, throw it out. The names with more pros than cons get put aside for later use. Not liking a domain or not seeing a future for it is an automatic throw away. If you don't do this now you will do it later when you have already paid for it.

5.) Number Your List of Possible Domains

Put your remaining list of domains in order starting with 1 as your favorite descending to your least favorite.

6.) Search For Available Domains

Go to GoDaddy.com and use your list to search for available names starting with your favorite.

7.) Purchase A Domain Name

After finding an available adequate domain name, make your purchase and be sure to follow the directions in this section to avoid hidden fees.

Make certain these action steps are completed before proceeding to the next section.

You will need to be a domain owner before proceeding.

Section 2
Hosting

Why is Hosting So Important?

Hosting is one of the most important things to consider when building a website. Some hosts may limit the amount of activity on your website based on your plan. This can lead to a loss of sales and trust from your customers.

When considering a hosting service you want something that will provide plenty of bandwidth for what your site is going to offer or have the option to upgrade as your site grows. Scrutinize the company by finding out how others feel about their customer service and stability before making your decision.

Yes, hosting, like any other service, costs money. Most hosting services give you the option to pay as you go on a monthly plan or pay for an entire year up front. The good news is that hosting is fairly reasonable ranging from a starter package of ten dollars per month to a business package costing one hundred dollars per month.

I have been using HostGator for the past four years in conjunction with another service called Webfaction. Although some of my larger sites are not compatible with HostGator, it outweighs the competition with quality customer service, quick response times, and affordable starter packages with unlimited capabilities making it perfect for this book and its readers.

In this section we will be signing up to HostGator so we can home our domain name. Don't get intimidated by the monthly fees. The affordable starter package will be sufficient. What's $100 a year for a potential ROI of $1000 a month?

HostGator is a very user-friendly service that offers a ton of great features that will benefit you financially and save valuable time.

Make sure you follow along closely as we walk through the sign-up process step-by-step.

With that being said, let's get started by heading over to HostGator by typing

HostGator.com into your Internet browser's address bar.

Signing Up to HostGator

When you reach HostGator's home page, it will present multiple plans and packages to

choose from. View other available hosting plans by clicking the button toward the top of

the screen to see other available packages.

When you reach the section of available packages, there will be three plans at the top

from which to choose. The **Hatchling Plan** offers what you are looking for but only

allows you to host one domain, while the **Business Plan** offers private SSL & IP and a

toll free number.

SSL stands for secure sockets layer. It secures data transferred over the Internet. IP stands for Internet Protocol. It identifies the computer that is sending and receiving transferred data.

You may choose the **Hatchling Plan** and upgrade later if you want to host another domain. The **Business Plan** is optional for those who wish to have a private SSL & IP and a toll free number.

The toll free number offered costs each minute a call is connected.

For the purpose of this book we are going to select the **Baby Plan** located in the center of the three plans presented at the top. This plan is just right for what you need to create your first site with the option to add more sites in the future.

Click the **Order Now** button to confirm your selection and finish setting up your new account.

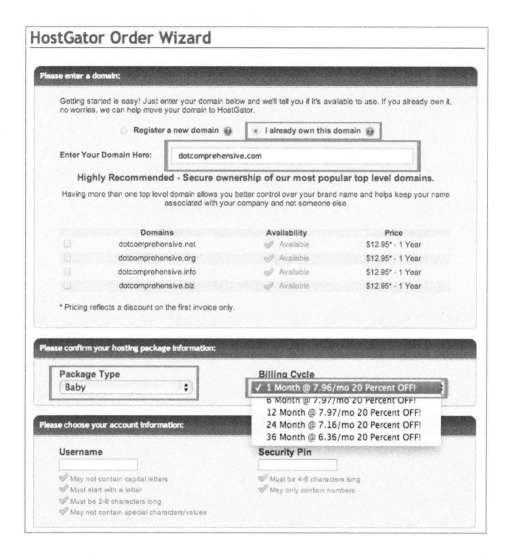

In the first box located at the top you will be asked to register a domain. Since you already nominated a domain for your product/website, it is unnecessary to register another one. Inform HostGator of this by selecting the box to the right stating you already own a domain.

When prompted to enter the domain you own, type it in with the chosen correct spelling. Make certain you type in the full domain followed by the extension you registered.

Extensions are what follow after your name, e.g., .com. For a full list of extensions and their meanings go to drbillbailey.net/extensions.html.

After you have given HostGator your domain information you may proceed to the section directly below it that asks you to confirm your package type and choose a billing cycle that will correspond with your budget.

The billing cycle is another commitment that you will face. Do you want to save a dollar every month and pay for three years up front or do you want to test your success first and make a smaller commitment? The decision is yours.

For the sake of testing, I am going to recommend that everyone select one month and opt to be billed monthly at $7.96.

Directly below your package information are two more forms where you will enter your username and a call-in security pin that will be used for account verification if you need to call customer support.

Next enter your **Billing Information** and add the method of payment, which will be billed to you based on your preferred billing cycle.

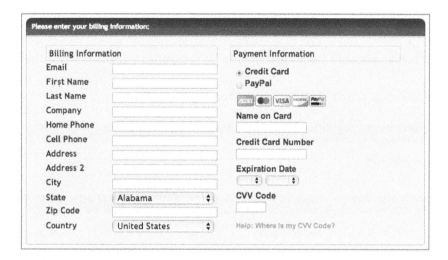

Use a credit or debit card that will still be active in several months so you don't have to change this information later. If you feel more comfortable using PayPal, the option is there. PayPal may be more appropriate for people with limited funds on their card.

Directly under the credit card form, you will see four boxes that contain extra features that are optional if you choose to pay for them. **SiteLock** and **CodeGuard** are selected by default. To save money, you may uncheck these.

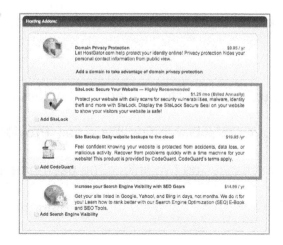

These features may be added at any time so don't feel obligated to add them now if you think it may be something worth trying in the future.

HostGator may have already provided you with a coupon. If one is not present, search Google and try various codes until one works.

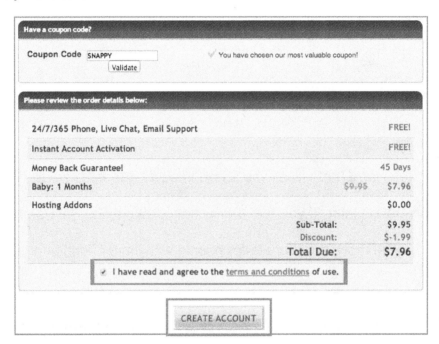

Check the box at the bottom that states: "**I have read and agree to the terms and conditions of use**" and review your information before finalizing your order. If everything is correct, click **Create Account** to confirm your order.

You will receive a confirmation email with your account details and login information. You may have to check your junk inbox to find this email. Provided will be two usernames and passwords, as well as two links. One username and password will be used for billing information linked to your account. The other username and password will be used for logging in to your cPanel account where you will manage your websites and domains associated with them.

Action Steps

1.) Sign-up to <u>HostGator</u>

Follow the directions in this section to properly set up a new <u>HostGator</u> membership. By doing so you will avoid extra fees for features and services we will not be covering in this book.

2.) Activate Your <u>HostGator</u> Account

Shortly after signing up to <u>HostGator</u> you will receive an email with your account information. Use the information provided in the email to activate and login to your account. If the email is not present, check your junk inbox.

If you currently have a service other than <u>HostGator</u>, make sure they offer cPanel to their members. If your current host does not provide a cPanel dashboard you may have trouble following along with some areas of this book.

Section 3
Name Servers

What Is a Name Server?

A name server is a computer server that hosts a network service for providing responses to queries against a directory service. Basically, a name server is responsible for linking meaningful names to IP addresses.

Locating Your Name Servers

At this point, you are done spending money. You should have everything you need to start the construction site: a domain for your product/website, hosting to give it a home, and the desire to build an authoritative site.

There is still one very important task to accomplish: changing the name servers within your GoDaddy account. You can't do anything with a domain name if it's in GoDaddy and you're in HostGator.

Before we get too far ahead of ourselves, we must first locate and record the name servers within your HostGator cPanel dashboard.

By now, you should have already activated your HostGator account by using the information provided by email after signing up for a new membership. If you have yet to complete this, do so now before moving forward.

Login to your account by clicking the link within the email and using the login information provided. Upon logging in, you will be acquainted with your new cPanel dashboard.

As you can see, there are an overwhelming number of features available to you, some of which we will discuss later in the book. Right now we want to locate our Name Servers.

The name servers are clearly displayed toward the bottom left under the account information box. It's the fourth column down, slightly larger than the columns above and below it.

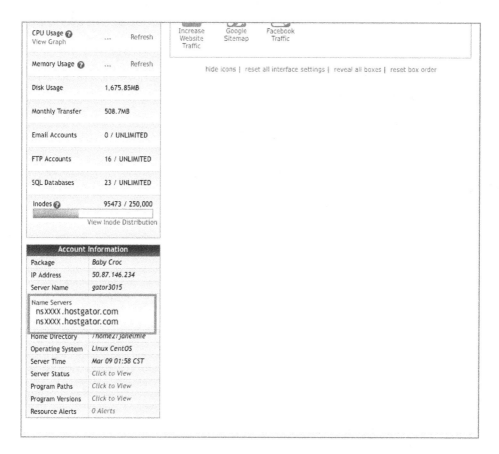

There are two name servers present on separate lines. Each line is a unique name server and should not be thought of as one.

Highlight them, one at a time, and press **Ctrl+C** for Windows users or **Command+C** for Mac users. Paste them on a separate local document on your computer by pressing **Ctrl+V** for Windows users or **Command+V** for Mac users.

Compare your name servers on the local document you created to the name servers in your cPanel account. Double-check and make sure they replicate the ones under account information.

Action Steps

1.) Login to Your HostGator Account

The email you received upon signing up to HostGator will contain your account information. Use the link provided within the message to go to your account login screen.

2.) Locate Your Name Servers

Your name servers can be found by scrolling to the bottom of your cPanel account home, four columns down under the account information box.

3.) Save Your Name Servers Locally

Highlight, copy, and paste your name servers to a local document on your computer.

If you are using a different hosting service other than what is taught in this book you will need to locate your name servers on your own. If you are having trouble locating them, a Google search will point you in the right direction.

Section 3.1
Name Servers

Configuring Your Name Servers in GoDaddy

With your name servers copied on a local document readily available, you are ready to make necessary changes in GoDaddy and give your domain name a new home. Don't stress this task. It is very simple and we are going to walk through the process together. So, stay close and pay attention!

Log in to your GoDaddy account by typing in your Internet browser's address bar GoDaddy.com and clicking the **Sign In** button, located at the top right of the screen.

Upon logging in, you will be redirected to your account home. Located at the top are your name, Customer Number, and Pin.

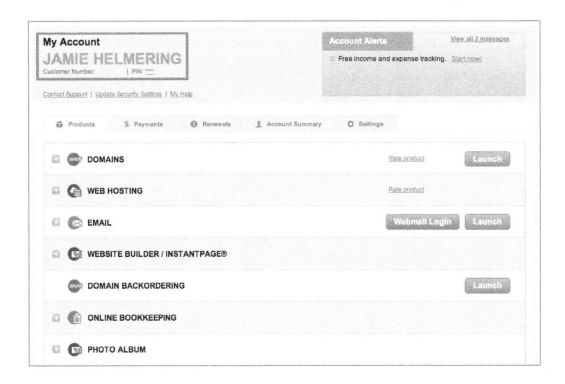

Within this menu you can manage all areas of your account including current and additional features. This is also the area where we will be modifying the newly purchased domain name.

To do this, locate the **Products** tab and find DOMAINS directly below it. Click the icon to reveal your current domains.

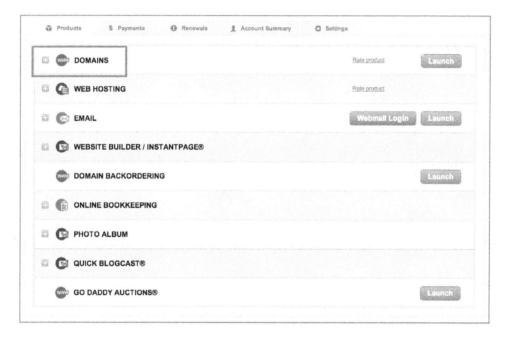

Presumably you have one domain on which to make changes. To the right of your domain is a **Launch** button that, upon clicking, brings up detailed information and settings.

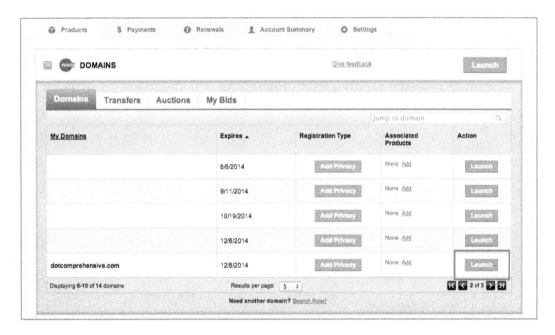

The initial page to which you are taken is where you will find the default name servers that you will need to edit. You will want to replace the current name servers with the ones in your local document. To do this, click **Manage**.

As you see, the set up type is set to **Standard** which means GoDaddy will be hosting it. Since you will be hosting this domain elsewhere you will need to select **Custom** and enter custom name servers.

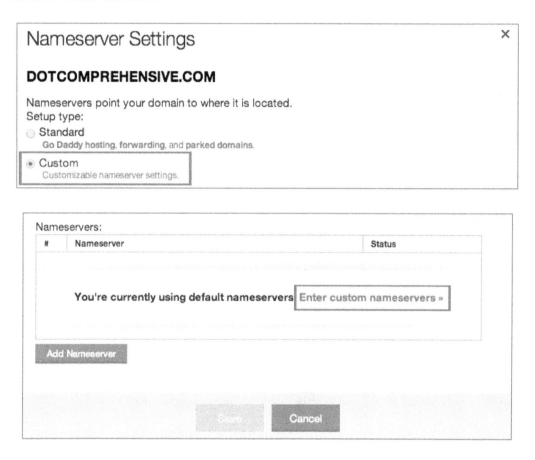

Enter your new name servers from your local document and make certain you only have one in each box. Click **OK** to confirm and save your changes.

Saving the new name servers exposes the domain settings page again. Don't be alarmed if the new changes are not present as it may take up to 48 hours for changes to take effect.

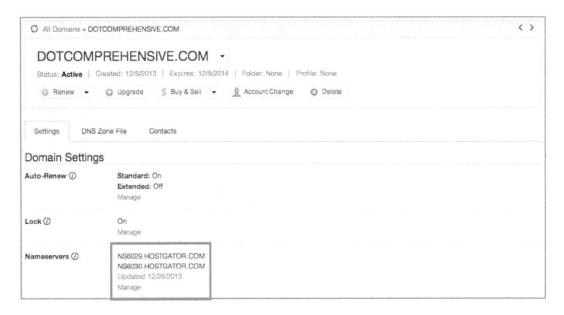

Clicking refresh often delivers the new settings for your name servers.

But it could still take up to 48 hours for the changes to be made in the backend side of

GoDaddy.

Shortly you will receive an email confirming the recent changes of your name servers. That's a green light to maneuver to HostGator and inaugurate the domain that is now pointing to your account.

Action Steps

1.) Log in to Your <u>GoDaddy</u> Account

Log in to your <u>GoDaddy</u> account by clicking the **sign in** button located at the top right.

2.) Launch Your Domain

In your account settings, navigate to the domains directly under the Products tab and launch your domain to make the necessary changes.

3.) Change Your Domain's Name Servers

Manage your domain's name servers by replacing the default name servers with the new ones that you saved on a local document. Apply the new settings and save your changes.

Before You Continue

Section 4 *explains the steps involved for adding* **_new_** *domains to your hosting account. If you will be building your website with the same domain name that was used to sign up to* _HostGator_*, you may proceed to section 5 of this book.*

Addon domains are for those who wish to create new websites.

Feel free to read it anyway.

Section 4
Addon Domains

Installing New Domains

Ultimately, you will want to create more sites and test different products you create or already possess. In order to do this, you will need to refer back to section 3.1 and revise your domain's default name servers.

After making the necessary changes in your domain account, you must inform HostGator of the transition before you can install software and other services on that particular domain.

To do this, log in to your cPanel account by clicking the link provided to you by email when you signed up to HostGator and locate the Domains category.

If you type in your Internet browser's address bar yourdomain.com/cpanel it will take you to your account log in screen.

Within the Domains category is the **Addon Domains** department that, upon clicking, grants you a form where you can add a new domain to your account.

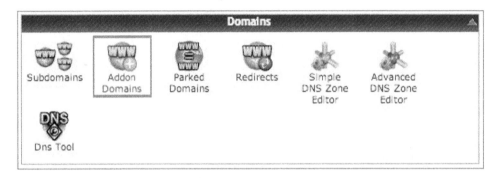

To add a new domain:

- Fill out all fields starting with your **New Domain Name** followed by its extension, e.g., yourdomain.com.

- Press **tab** twice on your keyboard to have **Subdomain/FTP Username** and **Document Root** fields generated automatically.

- Enter a memorable **Password** and double check that everything is correct before clicking **Add Domain**.

If you have properly filled out the required fields, a success message will emerge stating your addon domain has been created.

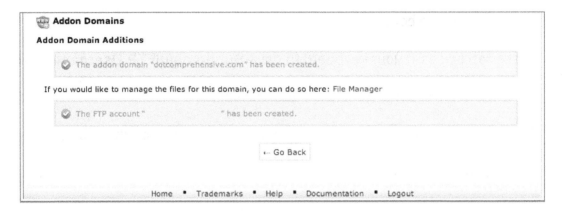

If you would like to verify that the domain was successfully added, use the

← Go Back **Go Back** button and look for your domain within the modify add-on domains section.

If everything appears to be correct, you may return to cPanel by clicking the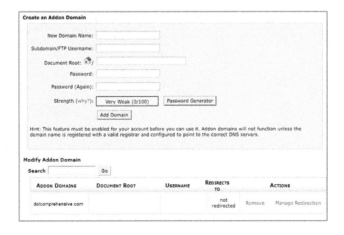

HOME icon located at the top left. If there are any mistakes, such as spelling errors, remove the domain under actions and repeat this lesson to make the necessary alterations.

Action Step

1.) Add Your New Domain

If you subsequently purchased a domain after signing up with <u>HostGator</u>, add it to your

hosting account in the **Addon Domains** section under the category labeled **domains**.

Fill out all fields using the **Create an Addon Domain** form and double check for typos.

If everything is correct, confirm it by clicking **Add Domain**.

Section 5
Installing WordPress

What is WordPress?

WordPress is an open source powerful content management system that offers a variety of features to users who want to develop a website, but have no prior web or programming experience.

The thousands of plugins and themes available for WordPress allow users to satisfy their site's appearance and functionality from within the admin panel. This revolutionary tool saves countless hours compared to conventional programming.

WordPress is especially acceptable for those who are on a budget, because most of the plugins in the directory are free for everyone's use. The themes available are free as well. However, the extent of the theme's features is very limited.

Conventional programming will obviously vanquish such a tool, but it comes with a steep learning curve. Creating a site may take you months of writing thousands of lines of code to make it function properly.

Don't rule out programming when starting your online venture. Learning a new language opens the door to many more opportunities. The possibilities for what you can achieve through programming are endless.

Installing WordPress on Your Domain

Because time is of the essence, we are going to keep it simple by using WordPress for our product. Keep in mind, it will likely be more than sufficient for your website.

Log in to your hosting account and ensure that you are in the cPanel menu. Locate the category **Software/Services** and click **Fantastico De Luxe**.

Fantastico De Luxe offers a large variety of features that you can install on domains within your account, including WordPress.

To begin the installation, locate WordPress in the navigation menu on the left side. Upon clicking, the screen to the right will display WordPress with large letters. Continue with a **New Installation** to bring up the install form.

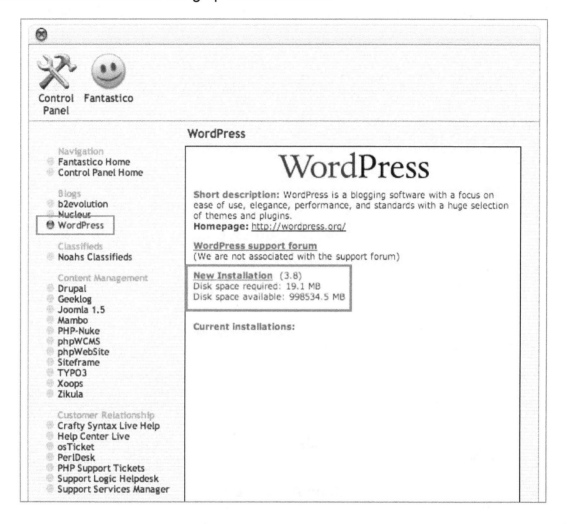

*The installation form allows you choose the **Installation location**,*

***Admin access data**, and **base configuration**.*

Follow the installation guide starting on the next page

to properly set up and install WordPress.

Installation Guide

Installation Location

Install on domain - Choose the domain name you want to install WordPress on.

Install in directory - The directory you want to make the installation on is the root directory. Leave this field blank.

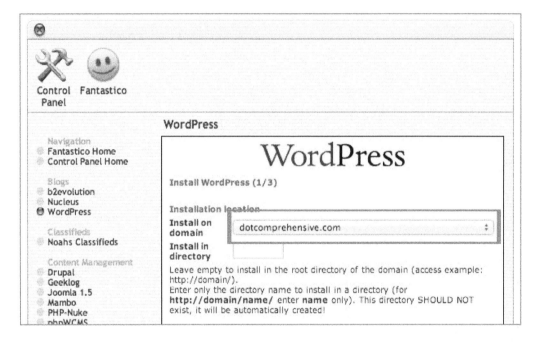

Admin Access Data

Administrator username - Create a username. You will use this name to access the admin panel of your WordPress.

Password - Create a memorable password for administrative access. This password will be the key for accessing your admin panel.

```
  phpWCMS
  phpWebSite
  Siteframe              Admin access data
  TYPO3                  Administrator-
  Xoops                  username     [            ]
  Zikula                 (you need this
                         to enter the
                         protected
  Customer Relationship  admin area)
  Crafty Syntax Live Help
  Help Center Live       Password (you [          ]
  osTicket               need this to
  PerlDesk               enter the
  PHP Support Tickets    protected
  Support Logic Helpdesk admin area)
  Support Services Manager
```

Base Configuration

Admin nickname - This name will show up when you make a post on your blog, rather than your admin username. This nickname keeps your login username hidden from others.

Admin e-mail - The admin email is used for multiple reasons such as username /password retrieval and various account notifications. You will be able to change this at any time within your WordPress admin settings.

Site Name - At this point, the site name can be anything, such as the name of your product because you will be installing a plugin that will override this. When you configure the plugin (discussed later), the name can be changed to something more appropriate.

Description - The description may also be anything such as, "The greatest site in the world." The same plugin that overrides the site name also overrides the description. Again, you may change it to something more appropriate when you configure the plugin.

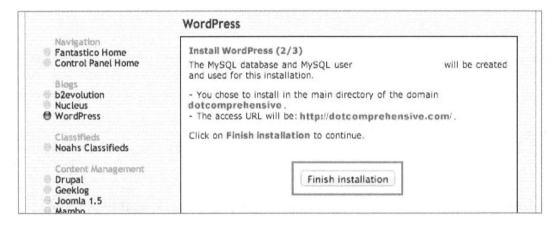

With the form properly filled out, click **Install WordPress**. This will bring you to a page that asks you to confirm your settings. Verify everything and click **Finish Installation**.

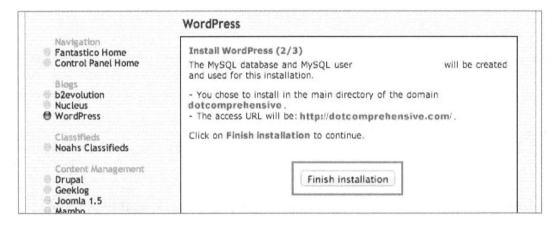

The install will begin executing files to your database and pause half way through prompting you for one more affirmation.

Some information may be blurred out for security purposes.

When it's finished, the installation overview will appear similar to the image below.

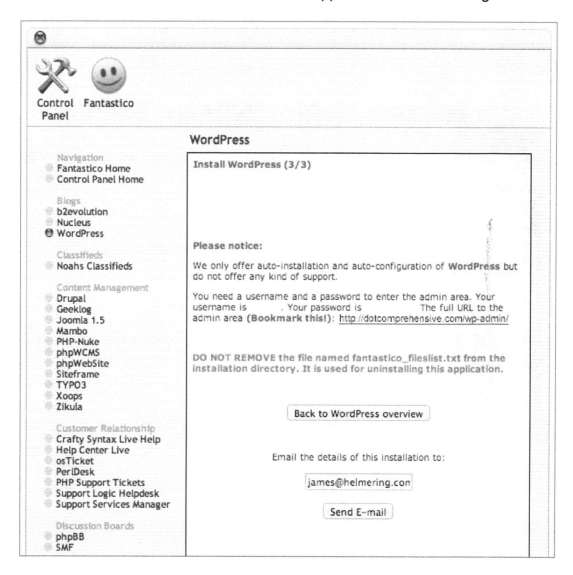

This form gives you the option to receive your account details by email. You can accept

the offer or return to **cPanel** by clicking **Control Panel** in the top left.

If the installation was done properly, you will be able to view your site by typing it into your Internet browser's address bar. It will feature a default theme with a sample page and blog post.

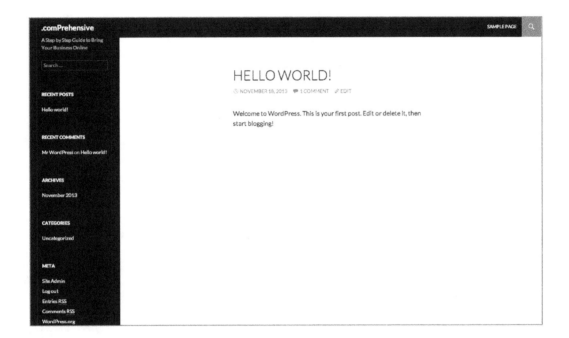

Action Steps

1.) Affix an Addon Domain to Your Hosting Account

Locate **add-on domains** under the category labeled **domains** in your cPanel home page. Follow the steps in this section to properly install your new domain.

2.) Install WordPress to Your Newly Added Domain

Locate **Fantastico De Luxe** under the category labeled **software/services** and follow the instructions in this section to properly install WordPress to your newly added domain name.

3.) Visit Your Site

Verify the installation was done properly by visiting it. The installation was successful if you see a default WordPress template similar to the one in this section.

Section 6
Business Email Addresses

What Is a Business Email?

Before you start personalizing your website, it's a good idea to have an email address that separates your business from your personal life.

A business email address is your website subsequently located after a user name of your choice e.g., support@yourdomain.com. Assigning such an email will establish an authoritative site and helps earn the trust of your customers when they are in need of assistance.

Signing Up to Microsoft Live Domains

Setting up a business email is easy to do. Google formerly offered a free email service for personal domains. But as of December 6, 2012 the free service was retired.

Fortunately, Microsoft is generous enough to provide a free service for personal domains, and it is surprisingly easier to set up compared to email set-up used by Google apps.

To create an email for a personal domain in Microsoft, type in your Internet browser's address bar domains.live.com and choose the link **Get started**.

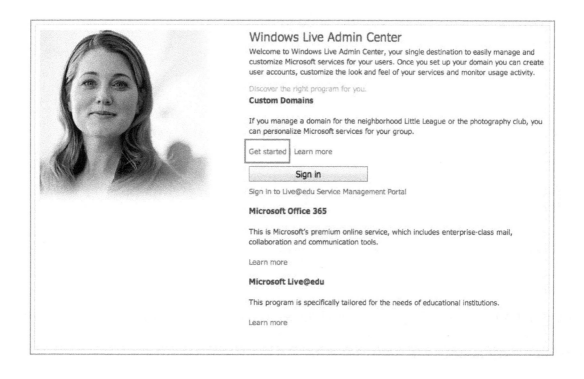

Next, you need to provide Microsoft with your domain name. Be sure to enter it correctly in the given field by adding the name followed by the extension, e.g., yourdomain.com.

Make certain the mail service for your domain is set up for Outlook.com and **Continue** to the next screen.

Before continuing any further, you will need to assign an existing Microsoft email to administer your domain.

Examples of Microsoft emails are @live.com, @hotmail.com, @outlook.com.

If you don't have an existing email with Microsoft, do **NOT** choose the option **Create a new Microsoft account in your domain**.

Stay on the current page and open a new tab by pressing **Ctrl+T** for Windows users or

Command+T for Mac users and register a new account at live.com. When you are

finished, return to administrator assignment page.

Once you have successfully registered a new Microsoft email address go back to Live

Domains, click **Continue**, and sign in to your account.

Upon signing in, you will see the details of your domain. After verifying the information is

correct, enter the security code and accept the terms applicable to your program.

Verifying Domain Ownership

For security purposes, Microsoft requires owner verification of the domain in which you wish to send and receive emails. When you have completed setting up your Microsoft live domain account, you will be taken to a page that presents you with information required for setting up email.

Microsoft makes the verification process very simple but the page can be quite overwhelming. Simply ignore everything except the top box under Mail Setup.

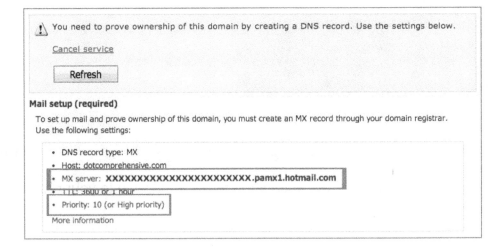

Within the Mail Setup box, you will need the snippet next to **MX server** and the number next to **Priority**. Everything else within that box can be forgotten.

Highlight the snippet next to **MX server**, and copy it by pressing **Ctrl+C** for Windows users or **Command+C** for Mac users. You may write the number down next to **Priority**, copy it as well, or keep it in the back of your mind.

The two pieces of information you collected will be copied to your hosting account. It tells HostGator that you will be using a different service to host your email.

This will require you to log in to your **cPanel** using the link provided to you by email when you initially signed up to HostGator or by typing in your Internet browser's address bar yourdomain.com/cpanel.

Upon logging in, you will need to locate the category labeled **Mail** and click **MX Entry**. Stay close as we walk through the proper setup guide to add a MX record for domain verification.

Before any changes are made, make sure the domain you want to set up email on is

selected at the top.

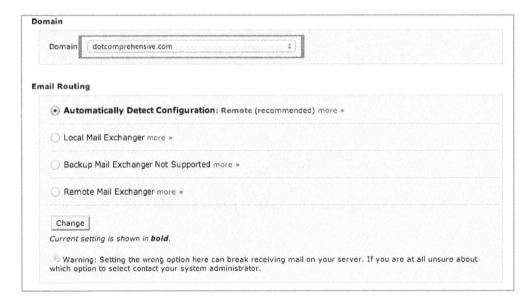

Using the information gathered from Microsoft live domains you will need to add a new

MX record in order to verify ownership.

Starting from the top locate the category labeled **Email Routing**. Most likely,

Automatically Detect Configuration is pre-selected. If it isn't, verify it yourself.

Did you remember to make a mental note of the **Priority** in your Microsoft live domain

account? This is the first entry you will need for adding a new record.

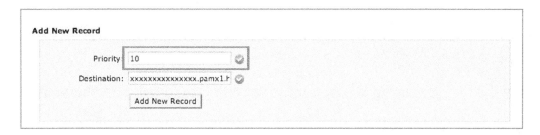

Directly below **Priority** is the **Destination** field. The snippet of code you copied from

your live domain account will be pasted here by pressing **Ctrl+V** for Windows users or

Command+V for Mac users.

When you add a new record it will appear at the bottom under the category labeled **MX**

Records.

Before you can successfully verify ownership of this domain within your live domain account, you need to delete the default MX record. To do this, click the **Delete** link underneath the **Actions** column and confirm your decision when prompted.

Verify that the only remaining **MX Record** is the one you added from Microsoft live domains. If everything is correct, you may log out of your account.

Your mail settings are unique to your account. Do not copy someone else's or use the ones in this example. The information shown in the images will not work for your account and should only be used as a reference.

With the new records successfully added to your cPanel account, you may return to your Microsoft domain administrator account.

Within your domain's mail set up is a large yellow box indicating proof of ownership is still needed. By clicking **Refresh**, Microsoft verifies that the MX records you added points to their server.

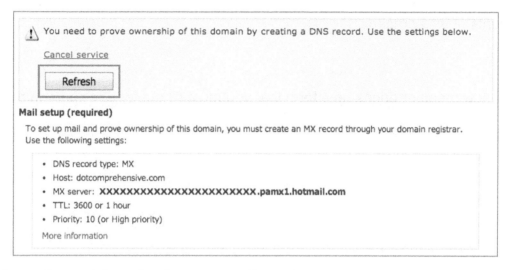

*Sometimes, it may take a few hours to verify and set up mail on your domain. If you still see the bright yellow box indicating proof of ownership is required after clicking **Refresh**, wait for a few hours and try again.*

A successful verification brings you to the **Member Accounts** area. Keep in mind, only the administrator can manage the members, with the outlook account assigned to your domain when you initially set up the account.

Adding Users to Your Domain

Setting up a user in Member accounts is pretty self-explanatory. Each member of your team can have his/her own email at your domain name for managing different departments of the company.

Adding a new member brings up a form that you must fill out for each person on your team. Microsoft allows you to add an exceptionally large amount of users, up to 50 accounts, which should cover all areas of your company.

A good rule of thumb to consider for your website is to have a general account for customer support. This is the first account you should create. Customize it to appropriately fit your site.

There are a lot of great account names you can use for customer support. I am typically accustomed to an account name such as **Support** or **Contact**.

This is your website! How you set up each email address

is for your determination.

Add an account	
Account name	Support
	The account name can contain only letters, numbers, periods (.), hyphens (-), or underscores (_).
First name	.comPREHENSIVE
	First name of the user displayed on web pages and in applications. This value is optional.
Last name	Support
	Last name of the user displayed on web pages and in applications. This value is optional.
Password	••••••••••••
	The password must contain at least six characters and is case sensitive.
Reenter password	••••••••••••
	☐ Require password change at first login
	OK Cancel

The above image shows "support" for the account name, which will establish the email

address support@dotcomprehensive.com.

When setting up a general customer support email address, use your website's name in the **First Name** field, followed by the department in the **Last Name** field.

When a customer receives an email, it will manifest the first and last name in that order, e.g., From - .comPREHENSIVE Support.

When creating a password for your account that you will be managing, it is unnecessary to assign a new one at first login. Simply **uncheck** the box before clicking **OK**.

The option to require password change at first login is optional for companies that will be adding multiple members for different departments. When checking this option, a temporary password is created by the administrator and given to the account member. Upon first logging in, the member will be required to change his/her password to something he/she will remember.

After adding the new member to your account it is ready for activation. Verify its existence under Account name and double-check it for any spelling errors.

If you will be assigning email addresses to other individuals on your team, this is the best time to do it.

Activating Your Business Email Address

With all members present and accounted for, sign out of the domain's administrator account and activate the assigned email addresses.

To activate the email you assigned to yourself in the domain's administrator account, type into your Internet browser's address bar: live.com.

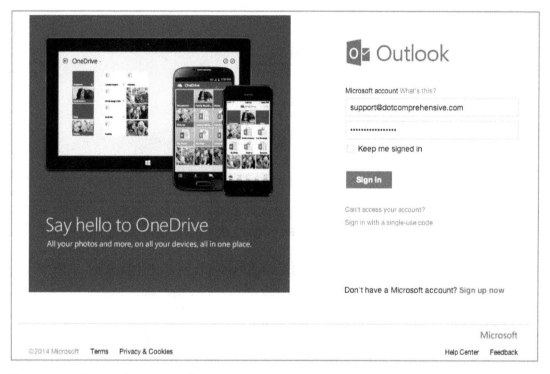

All users will need to go to live.com to sign in, activate, and manage their email.

At the login menu, use the account name you will be signing into followed by your domain, e.g., support@dotcomprehensive.com.

Logging in for the first time will require you to enter your date of birth, country and to accept the service agreement and privacy statement. Ensure you and your staff members enter correct personal information. Falsifying information has been known to cause problems, forcing the administrator to reset the account.

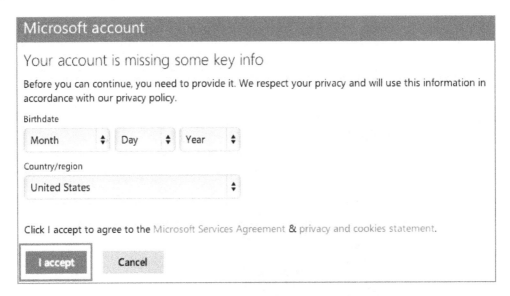

Clicking **I accept** will prompt you with a security code to verify you're human. By entering the security code and clicking **Continue**, you will have successfully activated your business email.

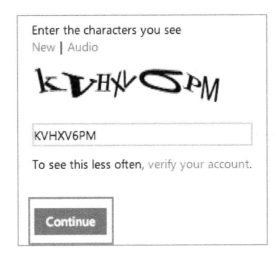

Testing Your Business Email

Now that you have successfully created an email for your website, it's time to take it for a ride. Testing everything you do, online related, is a good habit to form.

Sending an email through Outlook is a pretty straightforward task that corresponds with other email services you have probably used before. I am still going to walk you through this process so nobody is left behind. But I will try not to waste too much time.

When you activated your account in the previous lesson, you should have been taken to your inbox. Compose a new message to another email you manage to ensure that your account is working properly.

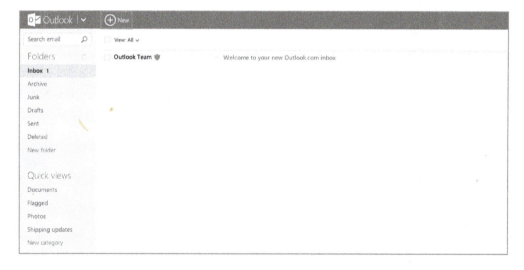

*Click **New** at the top to compose a new message.*

When you arrive at the composition form, test all fields by giving it a subject and message. Enter an email address that will have the honor of receiving the first email from your business account and send it using the link above your name.

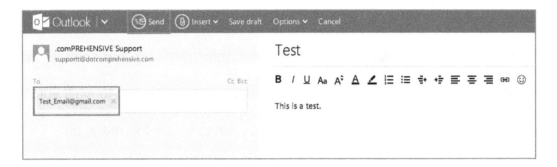

Check the email you sent the message to, including the junk folder. If it was sent successfully, your outgoing mail is working properly. Test the incoming mail in the same manner by replying to the email from within the account that received the email from your domain.

The tests ensure your business email address is operating correctly and ready to serve your website's customers.

Action Steps

1.) Sign Up to Microsoft Live Domains

Sign up to Microsoft Live Domains by going to domains.live.com and follow the on-screen instructions. Use an existing Microsoft account to administer your domain's email and member accounts. If you need to set up an account with Microsoft, go to live.com and create an account. Take note of your login credentials to prevent losing administrative access.

2.) Verify Domain Ownership

To verify ownership, use the MX record and priority that was given upon entering live domains. Login to your cPanel and enter MX records located under the category labeled **Mail**. Make sure the domain you are setting up mail on is selected. Enter in the priority number and paste the new MX record in the destination field. Delete the default MX record and verify ownership upon returning to your live domain account.

3.) Add a Member to Your Domain

Add a member to the account by filling out the new member form. If you need to add more members of your team, this is the best time to do so.

4.) Activate Your Email

Login to your new business account by going to <u>live.com</u>. Use your account name followed by your domain, e.g., support@yourdomain.com. Follow the brief on-screen instructions to activate your email address. Once the account becomes active you will be taken to your inbox.

5.) Send a Test Email

Test your account's outgoing mail and incoming mail by sending a test email to an account you manage and reply to it to ensure that it functions properly.

Section 7
WordPress Setup

Your Site at First Glance

The first time you visit your website, a WordPress template will be defaulted with example pages, posts, and links. This is a nice starting point and helps you see the possibilities of how your site could perform and serve the people who will be using it.

It's time to get that WordPress you worked so hard launching set up properly. In order to make any changes, you will need to be logged in to the Admin Panel.

Accessing Your Admin Panel

There are two ways to access your admin panel on a new WordPress. One way to do this is by locating the sidebar on the left and clicking the **Log in** link under the category labeled **META**. The other way to accomplish this task is by typing into your Internet browser's address bar: yourdomain.com/wp-admin.

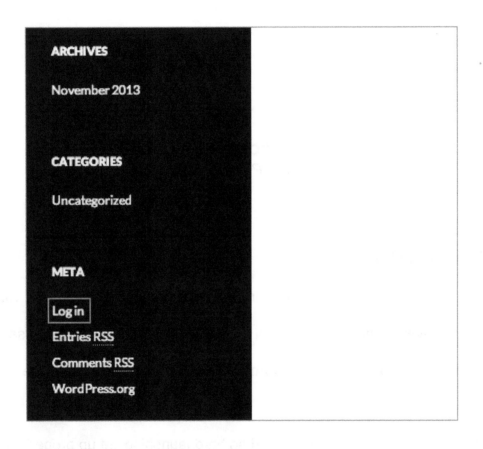

When you arrive at your website's admin login panel, you will need to enter the login credentials used when you first installed WordPress from within Fantastico De Luxe, as shown previously. If you have trouble remembering your login information, click the **Lost your password** link under the form, enter your email, and reset your password.

Upon logging in, you may be overwhelmed. There is a large quantity of categories and links presented and if you have never built a site before using WordPress, the initial perception can be deceiving.

Fortunately, the WordPress admin panel is very user friendly. Each element occupying the sidebar on the left was tailored for simplicity and designed to help individuals construct professional websites. These sections will be explained as we progress through the set up process.

Configuring Your Settings

The first thing you are going to alter is the general settings located at the very bottom. The changes you make within this section will make your site search engine friendly and influential.

Click **General**, under the **Settings** category, which brings you to your general settings. Some of these settings were established when you first installed WordPress from within Fantastico De Luxe, such as the **site title**, **tagline**, **URL**, and **email address**.

The "WWW" Prefix

Let's begin making some recommended changes to the URL structure of our site's address. Currently, your site's URL will appear in the browser's address bar as http://yourdomain.com/. A more appropriate and professional look, in my opinion, has the World Wide Web prefix that would make your URL appear as http://www.yourdomain.com/.

In order to make this alteration, you will need to edit both the **WordPress Address (URL)** and the **Site Address (URL)**. Simply add **www.** after **http://** but before your site's name.

While you are in this section, substitute the email address with your new business email.

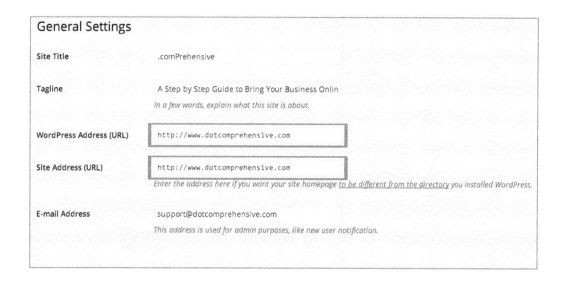

After adding the new prefix scroll to the bottom, click **Save Changes**, and be prepared to log back in. Your site should automatically log you out and refresh in order to serve the new prefix. If it doesn't automatically do this after saving changes, log out of your account and refresh manually.

Proper URL Structure

After being logged out and ensuring the prefix has been added to your URL, log back into your WordPress admin panel. This time we are going to change the appearance of the URL structure.

The default URL structure is set up in a way that is not appropriate for a website's search engine ranking. When search engines crawl your site, they determine where it should be located in their rankings according to how relevant it is in correspondence to particular keyword phrases users type in.

The algorithms that search engines use to determine relevance of a site and/or pages within a site may never be released to the public. However, search engines, such as Google, give out plenty of great tips to implement on our sites. We can also learn from other web marketer's trials and mistakes to enhance our site's authority.

One clearly effective method to improve a site's ranking is by implementing what some call, pretty links. Pretty links show the names of a page and/or post titles in the URL of a site instead of its ID. This is known as Post Name in WordPress.

Let's say your site is configured for post name and someone visits your contact us page. The URL in their browser's address bar will appear as yourdomain.com/contact-us.

Take that same situation, however, this time your site has the default URL structure. Now when someone reaches your Contact Us page, the URL in the browser's address bar will appear similar to yourdomain.com/p=001.

As you can see, there is a major difference between the default and the post type URL structure. Many tests have confirmed a website's page and/or post title, which appears in the URL, will likely rank higher in the search engines compared to a site that uses a default URL structure such as a page or posting ID due to relevance.

In order for us to make these alterations to the URL structure, you will need to locate **Permalinks** under the **Settings** category. There are various URL structures to choose from in this area.

Without a doubt, Post Name accommodates a relevant URL structure. The numeric structure does not meet our requirements for search engine rankings and the custom structure will not be discussed to avoid confusion.

What about the URL structure's day/name and month/name? Both of these permalinks show the title of the page in the URL. The fact is, although this URL structure will show the page title, the article is dated within the URL. Which means, each day the URL will age until it becomes stale material.

If your page with a dated URL ranks on the first page of a search engine, you will get fewer and fewer clicks as time moves forward because people don't want to read material that is outdated. Eventually, the search engines will catch up to you and your page's rank will descend until it is obsolete. The only time you should really consider a dated URL structure is when creating a website that receives consistent news updates.

There is a reason for changing your URL structure before you start adding any content to your site. If a search engine starts ranking the pages within your site and you change the structure of the URL after the matter, those URLs will no longer work. With that being said, select Post Name for the permalink structure within your settings and click **Save Changes** at the bottom.

Common Settings	
Default	http://helmering.com/?p=123
Day and name	http://helmering.com/2014/03/09/sample-post/
Month and name	http://helmering.com/2014/03/sample-post/
Numeric	http://helmering.com/archives/123
● Post name	http://helmering.com/sample-post/
Custom Structure	http://helmering.com /%postname%/

WordPress Plugins

The most incredible thing about creating a site with WordPress is having access to their 25,000+ plugins directory.

Each new plugin that's installed will appear on the left side of your admin panel where you can manage the settings or make necessary alterations in order to function properly for the site that it is installed on.

Some plugins may appear in different categories of the sidebar such as settings, tools, and other random areas. If a plugin is not seen in its own category once you have installed and activated it, do not get frustrated. It's only a matter of finding it by exploring areas within your admin panel.

What is a Plugin?

Plugins are an added feature that extends the functionality of your site. Almost anything you can imagine can be found in the WordPress plugin directory. Better yet, the majority of them are open source, meaning they're FREE!

Each plugin can be searched, installed, and managed directly from your WordPress admin panel making it simple to set up. The developer maintains the updates, removing bugs, glitches, and keeping it compatible with WordPress's updates so you can focus on the important areas of your site.

Pre-Installed Plugins

Before your mind runs wild with plugins that you want to add, locate plugins and click on installed plugins to see what is already available. Likely you will have two that come pre-installed with your WordPress called Akismet and Hello Dolly.

The first plugin, Akismet, protects your website from comments and traceback spam. It automatically gets sent to the Akismet server and runs through hundreds of tests to see if the comment is legitimate or spam. Activate Akismet by clicking the **Activate** link directly underneath it. Even if you're currently not accepting comments, you will be prepared when the time comes.

Before you set up your Akismet account, let's delete the unnecessary Hello Dolly plugin by clicking the delete link directly underneath it and confirming the decision on the next page.

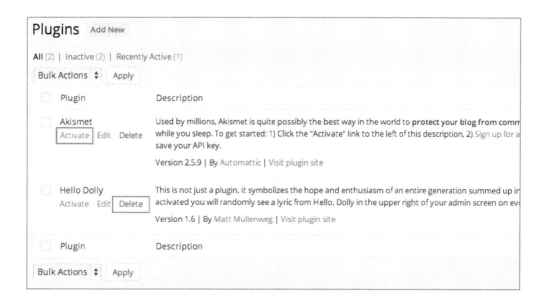

Hello Dolly serves no purpose. It randomly displays a lyric from the song 'Hello, Dolly' by Louis Armstrong at the top of every page of the WordPress admin area. It is considered to be something WordPress introduced to demonstrate what plugins could do, and today still comes pre-installed on every new install.

After deleting Hello Dolly you should only be left with Akismet and that annoying blue button prompting you to activate your account.

Let's begin setting up this first plugin by clicking the **Activate** button.

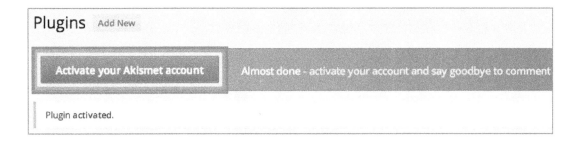

A new area within WordPress appears asking you to enter an existing key or add a new one. Click **Create a new Akismet Key**.

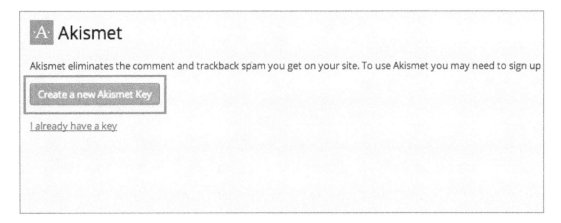

This will take you to the Akismet home page where you can set up your account and generate a new API key.

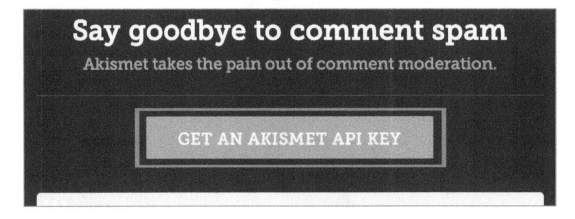

To create a new Akismet key, you must have a WordPress account. Most likely, you do not possess one yet. So let's create one together within Akismet.

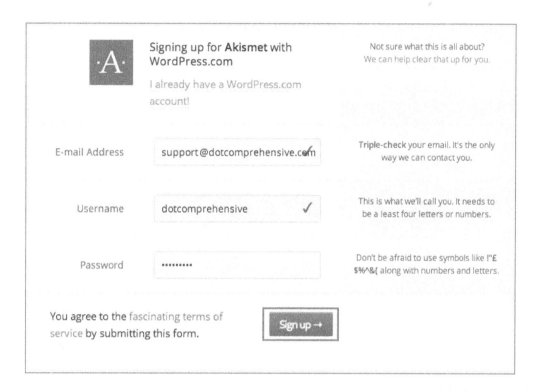

This is NOT your website's admin ID and password. This is a separate account that you must create from within Akismet or by going to Wordpress.com.

Make sure to enter a valid email address because you will need to verify it. Why not sign up using your awesome email @yourdomain.com?

When you click **Sign up**, check your inbox and verify your account.

Akismet may require you to verify your email address before continuing. But often you will be re-directed to a subscription page after clicking **Sign up**. Once you reach the subscription page, select the plan to the left for Personal Blogs/Single Websites.

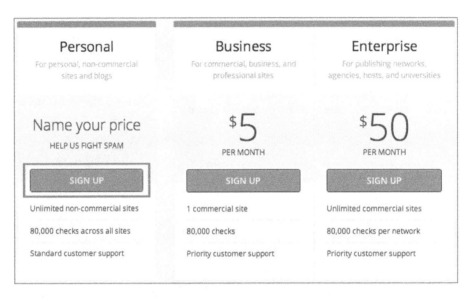

Selecting the free plan will take you to the final step where you are, once again, asked to make a contribution to Akismet. However, by sliding the contribution amount to zero you won't have to pay anything. Enter your first and last name and **Continue**.

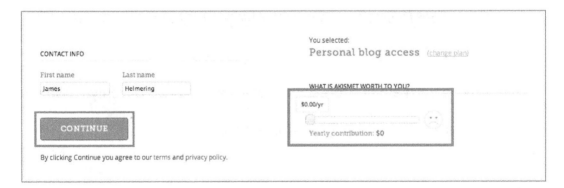

Finally, you will reach a success page giving you access to your new Akismet API key.

You will also receive an email containing the API key as well.

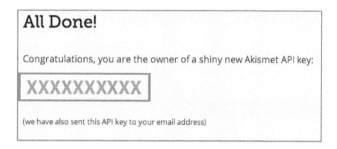

Copy the given code by highlighting it and pressing **Ctrl+C** for Windows users or

Command+C for Mac users.

Go back to the Akismet plugin within your WordPress admin panel by locating plugins

and clicking on **Installed Plugins**.

Again, click the big blue button that says **Activate your Akismet account**. This time

instead of creating a new key, you are going to click the link stating you already have

one.

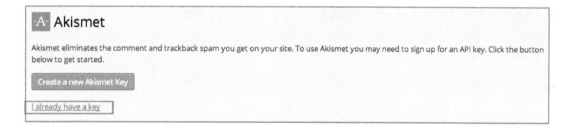

Paste your newly created API key by pressing **Ctrl+V** for Windows users or

Command+V for Mac users.

Save your changes to be redirected to the Akismet settings with a success message at the top.

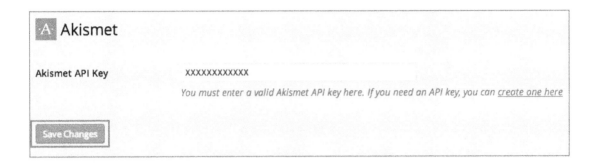

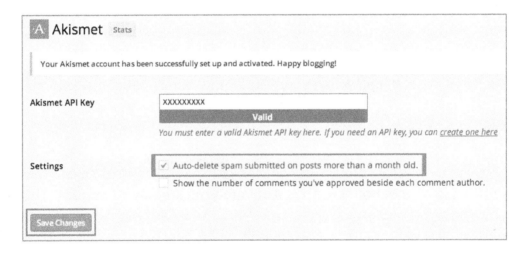

Within the settings, make sure the box is checked that tells Akismet to automatically delete spam submitted on posts more than a month old and save your changes. Once again, a success message will appear, and your Akismet plugin is now set up and ready for use.

Akismet is just one useful plugin that is available to you. It comes pre-installed with every WordPress. It runs inconspicuously in the background of your site and greatly reduces the amount of time it takes to monitor spammers.

Installing New Plugins

There is a solution to almost everything in the WordPress plugin directory. You just have to know what you want your site to do.

This book was written to ensure that you could easily create and manage a successful site. Together we will walk through and install great plugins that play a major role in a successful site.

Sure, you may have another feature in mind that isn't covered in this book, but by the time you are done with this you will have the knowledge to search and install other plugins that you need in order to accomplish desired tasks. So, worry not!

Running a business requires customers, correct? However, you may think that paying for traffic is too risky and word of mouth just isn't enough. Which is why being found in the search engines for free is a wonderful way to generate traffic and revenue. Luckily, there is a plugin for everything.

All in One SEO

All in One SEO is a free plugin that will optimize your site for success. With it, your site will move right up the rankings in the search engines, whether you have been building sites for years or just starting out. All in One SEO is for you.

This will be the first plugin we install that doesn't come pre-installed with new WordPress sites. It's a little bit of a different process but I promise, just as simple.

In order to install this and future plugins, you will need to search the WordPress plugin directory. To do this, locate plugins on the left of your admin panel and click **Add New**, directly under installed plugins.

Within this area is a search box where you can discover thousands of useful plugins. You don't necessarily need to know the name of any plugin; you just have to know what you want your site to feature. Typing in keywords related to the feature you need or want will bring up a selection of plugins from which to choose.

Since we already know the name of your first plugin, All in One SEO, there is no need to type in keywords. But, if I hadn't recommended this, you may have searched keywords such as seo, search engine optimization, or a keyword phrase such as rank in search engines and found this plugin by yourself.

Knowing that, type in the search box "All in One SEO pack" and click the **Search Plugins** button to the right of the form.

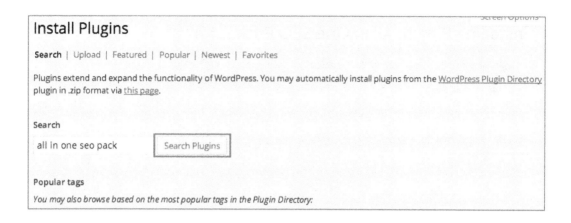

The plugin's database displays multiple plugins relevant to your keywords, placing the most relevant at the top. Locate the All in One SEO plugin and click the **Install Now** link directly below it.

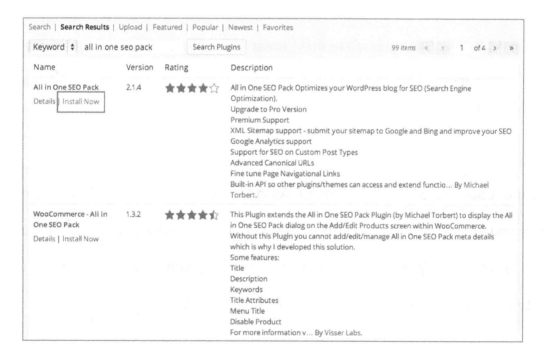

Wait as WordPress downloads, unpacks, and installs the plugin from its database automatically.

Installing Plugin: All in One SEO Pack 2.1.4

Downloading install package from https://downloads.wordpress.org/plugin/all-in-one-seo-pack.zip...

Unpacking the package...

Installing the plugin...

Successfully installed the plugin **All in One SEO Pack 2.1.4.**

Activate Plugin | Return to Plugin Installer

Click **Activate Plugin** to be taken back to the plugins manager with the new plugin displayed, ready for set up.

You will repeat this process each time a new plugin is needed.

To set up All in One SEO you will need to enter the settings of the plugin. Locate the plugin on the left toward the top of your admin panel and enter the General Settings area.

When you reach the General Settings for All in One SEO, scroll down to the homepage settings and enter in a homepage title, description, and no more than seven keywords relating to your site. Upon completing this task click the button **Update Options** located at the top and bottom of the page to confirm your SEO settings.

We already did this in Fantastico De Luxe, minus the keywords, but I mentioned it wasn't as important and this is why. All in One SEO overrides everything you entered prior to this step.

Your title should be a max of 60 characters and your description a max of 160 characters. Enter a max of seven keywords relating to your site, separating them by a comma. Any more than seven keywords and your site will become too broad and less relevant.

If you haven't already, get several up-to-date books about search engine optimization. Learn all that you can because this is how free traffic is achievable and could save you thousands of dollars, if not more. Continue educating yourself on this topic because search engines are constantly making changes to their algorithm to ensure that the people clicking ads/making them money are happy with the results they get when doing a search.

There are just too many areas to cover on search engine optimization, and it would be extremely difficult to keep this book updated with recent changes. That's why it's best to find a program, book, or articles to read online and stay up-to-date on this subject as long as you're developing websites or, at least until your business is large enough to hire a full-time trained SEO employee.

Setting Up a Shopping Cart

It's time to set up a shopping cart so you can sell and get paid for the products on your site. But first, you need to determine which form of products will be available to purchase.

Do you have downloadable products such as software, digital books, pictures, movies, etc.? Or do you have physical products such as items that need to be shipped when someone completes a transaction?

WP Marketplace - Physical Products

If you are going to be selling physical goods, I recommend WP Marketplace. It's a great plugin that allows you to add multiple products along with detailed information including cost, weight, dimensions, discounts and much more. This plugin makes it easy for your customers to add items to their cart and check out when they are finished.

Within the settings you can customize overall details that your customers will want to know, including shipping costs, tax rates, coupon codes for special events or holidays, and more.

When a customer is ready to check out, he or she will be asked for shipping details and contact info prior to completing a transaction. As soon as a transaction is complete, a new order will appear in your site's admin panel along with the customer's details. This leaves you with one task... shipping and handling.

Once you install and activate WP Marketplace, you should go through each setting and edit it according to your desire. You have the option to accept three different forms of payment, which include PayPal, Google wallet, and Cheque. If your company ships locally, the option to accept cash on delivery is also available.

Although WP Marketplace is great for physical products, it's a bit too much for selling digital items. Does it allow you to sell digital goods? Yes, but unfortunately your customers are required to enter too many personal details, which are not necessary for digital goods. This can often lead to skeptical buyers, resulting in the loss of sales.

If you are selling digital goods such as e-books, software, or media, your customers are going to want to click Buy Now, enter their credit card information, and instantly download the product. That is why I recommend a plugin dedicated for digital goods.

Search WP Marketplace and Install/Activate for eCommerce websites.

Easy Digital Downloads - Digital Products

Selling digital goods is one of the quickest and easiest ways to generate a decent income online. Digital products also free up a lot of your time compared to physical goods. Create a valuable unique product, one time from your computer, and sell it to people in need of it over and over again. There is no shipping required, and everything is automated. All you have to do is collect a check and ensure customer satisfaction.

Easy Digital Downloads is perfect for digital goods. It protects your products by blocking the download pages and ensures that the customer completes a transaction before receiving a unique download link that they will not be able to share with friends.

This plugin is totally customizable, providing you with everything you need for selling digital goods, The Right Way!

Multiple products can be added, and the stats help you make necessary changes to your sales pages to increase profits.

Search Easy Digital Downloads and Install/Activate for managing downloadable products.

The vast majority of features in WP Marketplace and Easy Digital Downloads are self-explanatory. However, taking some time to understand how they work is a wise thing to do. Add products and make test sales using promo codes and other various settings to ensure everything is working properly before announcing your site to the world.

Some plugin features might not look right when viewing them with the WordPress default theme. Don't get frustrated! You will be able to retest the plugin when we change your Theme in the upcoming pages.

PC Hide Pages - Hiding Specific Pages

PC Hide Pages is a plugin that lets you hide specific pages from visitors and search engines such as your thank-you pages. By selecting the pages you want hidden in the settings, it will no longer appear in standard menus, lists, or searches. It also adds a no follow code to prevent search engines from indexing pages you choose.

The pages you hide are still accessible, but you will be responsible for guiding a visitor to that particular page, such as your thank-you page. When setting up the plugin that manages your site's products, you can redirect your customers to a thank-you page upon completing a transaction.

Before publishing a page within your admin panel, a two selection drop down box will allow you to select **yes** for hiding the page or **no** for keeping the page visible throughout your site and possibly indexed by search engines.

Search PC Hide Pages and install / activate to hide pages visitors do not need to access right way, if at all.

Broken Link Checker - Find Broken Links Before They Do

Broken site links could lead to a loss of sales and a lower ranking in the search engines. It is very important to know if everything on your site is working 100%. However, as your site grows, so do the number of pages and links.

This could take an enormous amount of time to consistently check links and ensure proper functionality. The Link Checking plugin monitors your site and will notify you of the error in the admin panel or by email. This will give you time to do more important things on your site such as managing sales.

This plugin is very easy to set up. Search, install, activate, and forget about it until it informs you of a broken link within your site.

Search Broken Link Checker and install / activate to ensure your site never has a broken link that could potentially damage sales.

WassUp Real Time Analytics - Analyze Visitor Traffic

Wouldn't it be nice to know every time someone visits your site and how he or she found it? This can be achieved with the help of WassUp Real Time Analytics. It monitors visitor traffic in real time and records detailed information, which can be used to increase sales. No, it's not spying software.

The information recorded includes common details most companies try to acquire in order to understand their customers and what they want. Some of these details include the type of computer being used, general region, and which site or search engine referred them.

Knowing which type of computer the majority of your customers are using, such as Mac or PC, can help you identify product compatibility.

If you are only receiving sales within the English speaking territory, you could consider converting your product to another language. If you are only getting referrals from Google's search engine, perhaps you could increase your sales by learning what other search engines such as Bing and Yahoo look for when ranking sites. This plugin requires no set up. Just search it, install and activate it and watch your visitors as they explore your site.

Search WassUp Real Time Analytics and install/activate to analyze site traffic.

Zopim Widget - Communicate With Potential Customers

The Zopim plugin allows you to engage your visitors and increase conversions. With this plugin you can identify the page your visitors are on and start a conversation. This conversation may just be that little push he or she needed to be converted from a visitor to a customer.

Zopim also allows your customers to start an instant conversation with you by clicking the chat box located at the bottom of their screen and typing a message. If you are not available / signed in to Zopim, your status will be shown as offline. Your visitors may leave a message, which will be instantly emailed to you upon submitting the form. The email will contain your visitor's email address and message ensuring you will never lose a customer on your days off.

One of my personal favorite features of Zopim is being able to stay in touch with my visitors using my smart phone. It works on both iPhone and Android platforms, free to download and use. Prior to leaving your office, sign in with your smart phone and it's like you never left.

Once you install and activate this plugin you will need to register a new account by clicking the newly installed plugin on the left side of your WordPress admin panel and clicking Account Set Up in the drop down menu. You will be asked to link a current account or sign up. Click **Sign up now** at the bottom.

Set up your Zopim Account
Congratulations on successfully installing the Zopim WordPress plugin! Activate an account to start using Zopim Live Chat.

Link up to your Zopim account

Zopim Username (E-mail)

Zopim Password

Use SSL   ☐ uncheck this if you are unable to login

The Zopim chat bar will displayed on your blog once your account is linked up.

[Link Up] Don't have a zopim account? Sign up now.

The **Sign up now** link brings you to Zopim's website where you can begin the sign up process.

The email address you use will be the portal for which messages are received when you are unavailable. It will also be used to activate your account following the form submission.

The completed form will send you an email with the Zopim activation link. This link redirects you to a form where a password will be chosen.

After choosing a password, complete your profile by entering a first, last, and display name. The display name is what your customers see when communicating with you. Since you are using Zopim free, it is recommended to choose a general display name that will work for all people on your team.

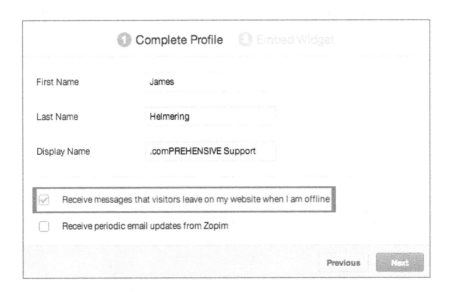

Another recommendation is that you choose the option to receive messages from visitors when offline.

The next section gives you a code to copy into your site's HTML. Since we are using WordPress, ignore this step. By installing the plugin, the code is automatically added where it is needed.

Now head back to your WordPress admin panel where we first started setting up the Zopim account. This time you will enter your email and the password you used to register to Zopim and click **Link Up**.

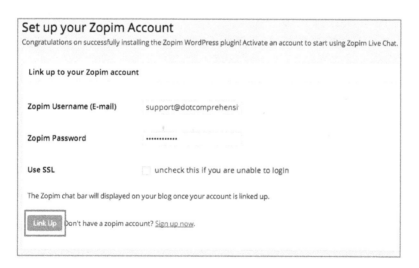

When you click the **Link Up** button, Zopim will show up on all pages within your WordPress. However, to be available for chat, you must be logged in.

To log in, locate the Zopim Chat plugin on the left side and click the Dashboard link. Within the dashboard, you can log in and communicate one-on-one with your visitors.

Search Zopim and install/activate to communicate to your visitors one-on-one.

That concludes the WordPress first-time set up. Make sure your installed plugins menu mirrors the image below. If you sell both physical and digital products, you should try to utilize both the WP Marketplace and Easy Digital Downloads plugin for an easier buyer experience.

Plugin	Description
Akismet Deactivate Edit Settings	Used by millions, Akismet is quite possibly the best way in the world to protect your blog from comment and trackback spam. It keeps your site protected from spam even while you sleep. To get started: 1) Click the "Activate" link to the left of this description, 2) Sign up for an Akismet API key, and 3) Go to your Akismet configuration page, and save your API key. Version 2.5.9	By Automattic	Visit plugin site
All In One SEO Pack Deactivate Edit	Out-of-the-box SEO for your WordPress blog. Options configuration panel	Upgrade to Pro Version	Donate	Support	Amazon Wishlist Version 2.1.4	By Michael Torbert	Visit plugin site
Broken Link Checker Deactivate Edit Settings	Checks your blog for broken links and missing images and notifies you on the dashboard if any are found. Version 1.9.2	By Janis Elsts	Visit plugin site
Easy Digital Downloads General Settings Deactivate Edit	Serve Digital Downloads Through WordPress Version 1.9.8	By Pippin Williamson	Visit plugin site	Getting Started	Add Ons
Link to Your Content Settings Deactivate Edit	This plugin gives you an easy way to link to your media library, posts, pages, custom post types and taxonomies. Version 1.7.2	By Ray Milstrey	Visit plugin site
PC Hide Pages Settings Deactivate Edit	Allows you to hide pages from WordPress menus, blog searches and search engines. Version 1.4	By Peter Coughlin	Visit plugin site
WassUp Real Time Analytics Deactivate Edit Settings	Analyze your visitors traffic with real-time stats, charts, and a lot of chronological information. Includes a sidebar widget of current online visitors and other statistics and an admin dashboard widget with chart. For Wordpress 2.2 or higher. Caution: don't upgrade when your site is busy! Version 1.8.4	By Michele Marcucci, Helene Duncker	Visit plugin site
WP Marketplace Deactivate Edit	WordPress Marketplace is a free full featured Shopping Cart / eCommerce Plugin with everything you need on an easy UI, to build eShop or marketplace. Version 2.3.6	By Shaon	Visit plugin site
Zopim Widget Deactivate Edit	Zopim is an award winning chat solution that helps website owners to engage their visitors and convert customers into fans! Version 1.2.7	By Zopim	Visit plugin site
Plugin	Description

Action Steps

1.) Configure Your Site's Settings

Log in to your WordPress admin panel and familiarize yourself with its functions. Make the necessary changes in the settings, which should include the www prefix, add your business email address, and configure your URL structure.

1.) Search, Install, and Activate the Necessary Plugins

Akismet

All In One SEO Pack

Broken Link Checker

Easy Digital Downloads - *For those selling digital goods.*

WP Marketplace - *For those selling physical products.*

PC Hide Pages

WassUp Real Time Analytics

Zopim Live Chat

2.) Add Your Product to The Marketplace

Add your product(s) to your site within the plugin that you will use for selling and shipping goods.

3.) Test Your Plugin's Functionality

Make sure all plugins are properly set up and working by locating and clicking them in your WordPress admin panel on the left side. Set them up by following the instructions in this section.

Some plugin features might not look right when viewing them with the WordPress default theme. Don't get frustrated! You will be able to retest the plugin when we change your Theme in the upcoming pages.

Section 8
Content Creation

Writing Relevant Content

Writing can be a boring and strenuous task, but you want your site's pages to rank high in the search engine, and in order to accomplish this, there are strict rules and guidelines to follow, often making this task time consuming.

Writing used to be difficult for me too. I used to sit at the computer for hours and only have one sentence written. Later, I found that I was making it harder than it actually was.

A while back, I took a course on content development that taught students to write their content in an unusual way. This unorthodox method of writing turned out to be the fastest and most effective way to create good quality content in a timely fashion.

In this section I am going to share this form of writing with you. It will save you time and, for once, make writing content fun.

Ten-Minute Speed Calligraphy

Our entire lives we have been taught to edit as we are writing. Yet, this form of writing is constantly scrambling our brains, causing us to lose focus on the topic about which we are writing.

Start a new word document or create a text file for each page you will initially add on to your site such as Home, About Us, Contact Us, etc. Save each file individually using a name that represents the page you are writing about.

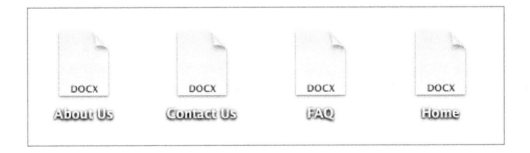

It is recommended to have these common pages on your site. You don't have to use the exact titles shown above, but you are more than welcome to do so.

When you write an article, the first thing you should do is outline each and every topic you will discuss. Once you have all of your topics laid out, your content practically writes itself.

Put all related topics in each page, leaving spaces for content/paragraphs. The topics will be the headline of each piece of content within your article. Your headlines should answer the reader's question before he or she has time to ask it. When you create headlines, ask yourself, "What are people going to say or ask when they come to this page?"

For example, if I were to present .comPrehensive to someone who doesn't have a website they would likely say:

"Why does my business need a website?"

"I don't have the money to spend on a website."

"I don't have any programming background."

"I am not computer savvy."

"I don't have a business, what would I sell?"

Those issues should be addressed in one simple line making it impossible for the readers to have any doubts, which will entice them to read more. With the pre-formed titles, it will be easy to stream through this article because I already know what to discuss.

.comPrehensive Home Page

The Importance of Online Presence For Businesses

How You Can Create A Website Without Spending A Ton of Money

No Programming Knowledge Required

You Don't Have To Be Computer Savvy

Make Money With Skills You Already Possess

Now that you have your titles laid out on individual pages, get out your timer and set it for 10 minutes. Yes, literally get out a timer either on your phone, stopwatch, or computer and free write. Continuously write anything that comes to mind without paying attention to grammar, spelling, or mistakes. This technique often produces ideas on the topic at hand, and prevents writer's block and self-criticism.

You can use an online stopwatch, found at www.online-stopwatch.com. This site has a countdown feature that uses an alarm to notify you that your time is up.

www.online-stopwatch.com

You can also move on to a different topic within your article. Once the 10-minute timer runs out, save the article, close it, and don't do anything to it for 24 hours.

Example of first ten-minute draft.

The Importance of Online Presence For Businesses

It is important to possess a website that reperesent s your company. A website can keep your business running round the clock secen says a week meaning the doors never close after hours.

A website also benefits business owners by allowing them to scale their products on a global scale which will not liomit your company to sell items in a general location.

How You Can Create A Website Without Spending A Ton of Money

There are lots of cost effective ways to bring a business online and plenty of tools available online to help you do so. However, they are often covered up by huge advertising campaigns geared towards website builders that lack in functionality and require you to purchase more and more packages to have a larger set of tools. These packages often run into the hundreds of dollars, when they are often free elsewhere.

No Programming Knowledge Required

Knowing a second language is beneficial in many ways but it its not necessaryiely required these days with the wonderful tools available online.

With open source tools, sucha s wordpress, you can build a professional website that commenerates your company and its' products.

You Don't Have To Be Computer Savvy

.comPREHENSIVE takes individuals by the hand who wish to posses a website, but lack the skills to create one. The details shown in this book are so thourgoughly explained that it would be hard to not follow along.

When I wrote this book I gave a copy to my friend, who can barley check his email, and had him create a website using the princlples taught. Just as the book claims, he was able to make a website.

Make Money With Skills You Already Possess

You don't have a business? So what! You likely already posess a skill that people are willing to pay money for which can be turned into a product. Skills such as crafting, gardenting, sewing, etc. can all be turned into high quality products such as How-to books or videos which you can sell on the website created by following this book.

It is very difficult at first to practice this technique if you are used to editing your article while writing, but after a little practice the mistakes made won't even be noticed.

This is not a trademarked writing technique. In fact, even some of the most successful authors use this method for writing books that you enjoy reading.

This form of writing prevents you from losing your train of thought by keeping your brain actively working on what to write next. By constantly stopping to fix errors within your article the brain begins to focus on errors, causing you to lose momentum. It may seem brainless and spontaneous but, if you think about it, this technique actually makes perfect sense.

After your first page/article has been written, reset the timer and go to your next document. Repeat this method of writing until all of your documents have "sloppy copies" and don't forget to save your work.

After all of your documents are completed and saved, forget about them because tomorrow is spring-cleaning. Don't even open them up to review your writing. Simply forget and return to them in 24 hours so your mind is fresh and full of new ideas.

Think about things you have written in the past. Have you ever written a last minute paper for school and before turning it in the next day, you took one final look at it and wondered what in the world was going through your head at the time of writing? You re-wrote it to make more sense right before class started and before your professor requested it to be submitted.

That is exactly what we are doing here. The only difference is that your professor won't be grading you; your customers will. You don't necessarily have a deadline to meet, but the sooner your site is complete, the sooner a check starts arriving in the mail.

Don't get too far ahead of yourself. Put this book down and return to your articles tomorrow then properly edit them before moving onto the next page/section of this book.

24 Hours Later

By following this step and practicing this writing technique, you will quickly develop content for your site. After 24 hours, begin reviewing your work and start editing, one at a time.

The material written may not be very good, but now you have something on which to base your fresh material. Now is the time to correct spelling errors, grammar mistakes, and rewrite any sentences that don't make sense.

Finalize your work to make it an outstanding, well written, one of a kind article that your customers and visitors will enjoy reading.

Example of finished article after 24 hours.

The Importance of an Online Business Presence

It is important to obtain a website that represents your company. A website can keep your business running around the clock seven says a week meaning the doors never close.

A website also benefits you, as a business owner, by allowing you to scale your products globally, which will not limit your company to selling items in a general location.

How You Can Create a Website Without Spending a Ton of Money

There are a lot of cost effective ways to bring a business online with plenty of tools available to help you do so. However, they are often covered up by huge advertising campaigns geared towards website builders that lack in functionality and require you to purchase unnecessary packages to have a larger set of tools. These packages often run into the hundreds of dollars, when they are available for free elsewhere.

No Programming Knowledge Required

Knowing a second language is beneficial in many ways, although it is not necessarily required these days with the wonderful tools available online.

With open source tools, such as WordPress, you can build a professional website that commemorates your company and its products.

You Don't Have To Be Computer Savvy

.comPREHENSIVE takes by the hand individuals who wish to possess a website, but lack the skills to create one. The details shown in this book are so thoroughly explained that it would be hard to not follow along.

When I wrote this book I gave a copy to my friend, who could barely check his email, and had him create a website using the principles taught. Just as the book claims, he was able to construct a website with zero prior knowledge.

Make Money With Skills You Already Possess

You don't have a business? So what! You likely already possess a skill that people are willing to pay money for which can be turned into a product. Skills such as crafting, gardening, or sewing, can all be turned into high quality products. How-to books or videos are a few examples, which you can sell on the website created by following this book.

We just did the four most common pages within a website. Repeat this process for every article you will be adding to your site and do not return to the next section of this book until each article has been written and edited.

Action Steps

1.) Lay Out All Initial Pages

Make a separate document for each page and save it locally to your computer's desktop or an easily accessible folder.

2.) Outline Each Page With Titles

Go through each document and outline the topics you will discuss for each page.

3.) Free Write

Set a timer for 10 minutes and write one article at a time until the timer runs out. Repeat this step for each document created.

4.) Ignore Your Articles for 24 Hours

Close out of your articles. Do not review, edit, or even look at anything you have written for 24 hours.

5.) Edit Your Articles

When you return to your documents after 24 hours, use the written material from the day before and finish writing your articles using a fresh mind to turn it into a work of art.

Section 9
Content Execution

Pages vs. Blog Posts

By now, you should be sitting on your own personal gold mine of well-written articles. Each of them dedicated to a specific page you wish to feature on your site.

Adding content to your site can be done through blog posts or pages. Blog posts are usually frequently added single entries made by a blogger in order to keep readers updated on particular subjects or matters relating to the blog.

Pages often contain related material to the site but are not updated as frequently as blog posts. They are used to navigate a website in order to gain knowledge about a particular product before making a purchase, which is relevant to what we are trying to accomplish in this book.

Deleting Unnecessary Pages

Pages in WordPress are self-explanatory. Log in to your WordPress admin panel by typing in your Internet browser's address bar yourdomain.com/wp-admin or by clicking the **Login** link under the category labeled **META**.

To the left of your admin panel, locate and click on **Pages**. Upon opening, you may notice there are already pages in there that you did not add. The page titled **Sample Page** is a default page that comes with every newly installed WordPress site. It is unnecessary and may be deleted.

To delete a page hover over it until you see four clickable options. Simply click **Trash** and the page will instantly be removed from the list.

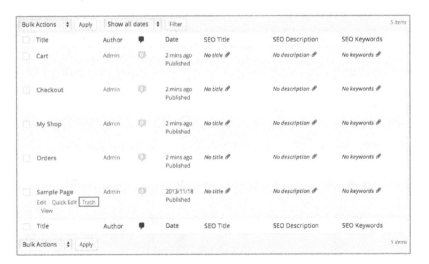

Although you deleted this unnecessary page from your list, it isn't gone forever. It goes to a trash folder similar to what you would find in your email account's inbox.

This allows you to restore a page if it is accidentally deleted. To do so, click **Trash** right above your list of active pages and then click **Restore**.

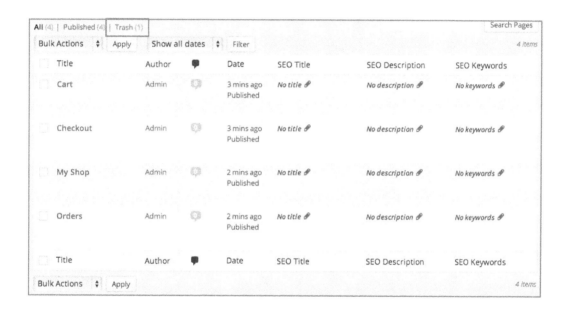

The Trash link will only show if there is a page within followed by the

number of deleted pages.

If you purposely delete a page, you may want to delete it from your trash as well because that same URL will be unavailable, if ever needed again, until this is done. To do this, simply go into your **Trash**, hover over the page you deleted and click **Delete Permanently**.

Uploading Your Fresh Content

Let's get back to adding the pages you just wrote.

Start with the first document you saved on your computer. Open it up, highlight everything within it, and press **Ctrl+C** for Windows users or **Command+C** for Mac users.

Return to your page menu within your WordPress admin panel and click the **Add New** button located toward the top of your page's menu.

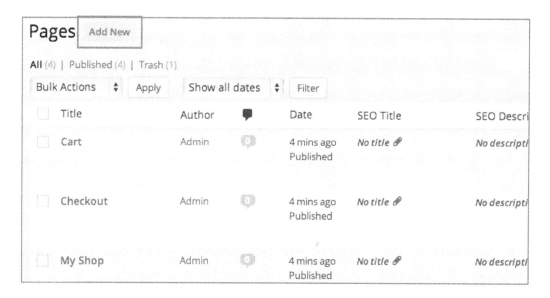

After adding a new page, you will be presented with a page form that displays various changeable settings. For now, only set up and explain the important settings or fields, which include your page title, permalink, content area, and the SEO plugin you installed.

For the title, choose a name that will represent the page and content you are adding. The title should be relevant to the content. For example, the first page I am going to add is my contact page. This will be the page that my visitors can reach me at, so I will call this page Contact Us.

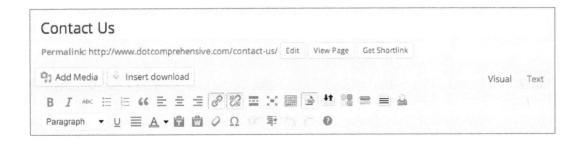

When WordPress was originally installed, you changed the permalink structure in your settings to show pretty URLs such as www.yourdomain.com/your-awesome-page instead of the default URL structure that would have looked similar to this: www.yourdomain.com/?p=1.

Ensure your permalink structure was set up properly by checking the URL under your page title once you have named it. If it was successfully changed, the URL structure displayed will contain your page title at the end of your domain's URL.

It is important to your visitors and search engines that your URL structure works this way because it will not be relevant as a URL that has /contact-us/ in it if a URL is /?p=1/ for your contact page.

If your URL structure doesn't look like the image displayed on the previous page, go to your settings and change the permalink structure of the post name.

Now paste your article in the content area by clicking anywhere in the content box and pressing **Ctrl+V** for Windows users or **Command+V** for Mac users.

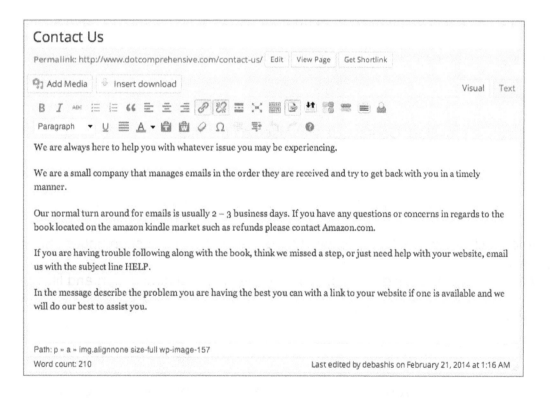

Now, you will finish this page by explaining and adding your home page title, description, and keywords to the SEO plugin that you have installed. Scroll to the bottom of the page to find the area that says All-In-One SEO Pack.

The **Preview Snippet** section, at the top of the screen is how your site will appear in the search engines for this particular page.

Next is the **Title** section. This is the first thing people see before they read your description and decide to click on your site. The search engines will cut it off after sixty characters, since this is the maximum number allowed, so be sure to have a clear title in sixty characters or less.

In the example provided, Contact Us was used as the title.

The **Description** gives a short but detailed description of your site and it is what consumers will see immediately following the title. Keep this section under 160 characters, or again, it will get cut off leaving only a partial description and likely resulting in a loss of visitors and possibly a loss of rank.

The last section is **Keywords**, which are words or short phrases that consumers type into search engines that describe a website, topic, or page and potentially lead them to your site. These keywords should be brief and strong to accurately identify your site and attract searchers. They should be in your website title and throughout its content. Using a large number of keywords may be tempting; however, it is important to limit the number of keywords used because using too many could have damaging effects. For example, it could lower your website's search ranking or flag it as a spam site.

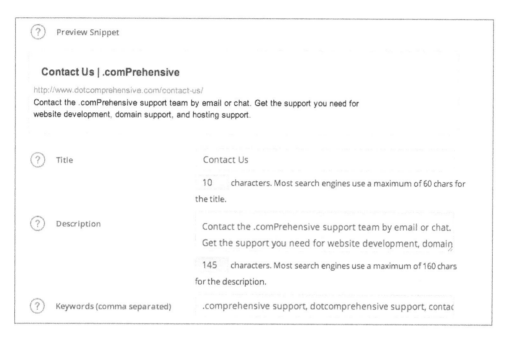

The SEO plugin you installed is one of the most important aspects of each page you add. It is imperative that you learn how to properly use this plugin and understand search engine optimization.

Even though this book does not go into much detail on SEO, it is one of the most important areas to learn in web development. Learn all you can in this area by reading up-to-date books or joining programs that keep up with the latest changes that search engines do to their algorithms.

Once you have everything completed properly on your new page form, take it live by clicking **Publish** at the top right corner of the screen.

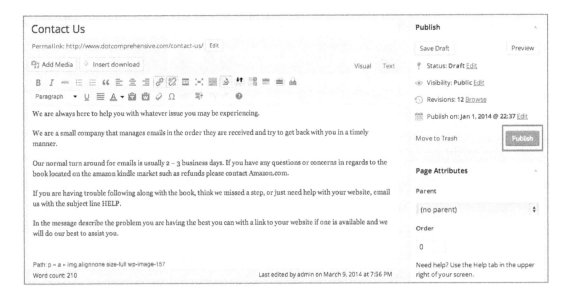

Repeat this process for each article you have written. Make sure your URLs match your page title and follow the guidelines mentioned in this section for properly setting up your SEO plugin.

The process used to add pages to the site are exactly the same for adding a new blog post. Create your title, paste in your blog's article, and properly set up your SEO plugin.

Removing Comments From Pages

There may be times that you don't wish to show comments on some of your WordPress pages or blog posts. This is something that can be fixed easily. If you want to disable comments on a page or post just simply hover over the page and click **Quick Edit**.

This will bring up a menu that allows you to quickly edit some of the page or blog elements, including the option to disable comments.

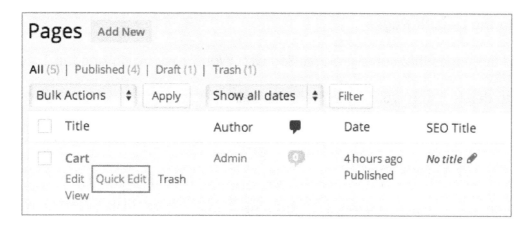

Uncheck **Allow Comments** and click **Update**. Once updated, the page or blog post will appear without a comment box below it.

Action Steps

1.) Delete the Default Pages

Delete all the pages that come pre-installed with WordPress by clicking the Trash link. Be sure to delete it from your trash menu as well.

2.) Add Your Website's Pages

Take the edited articles you wrote and add a new page. Enter a title relevant to your content, make sure your URL matches it, and copy the article in the content area.

4.) Set up Your All in One SEO Plugin

Properly set up your SEO plugin by ensuring the title is within 60 characters and the description is within 160 characters. Make sure that everything is relevant to your page and that you limit the number of keywords. Remember, use a small number of keywords which are unique, yet relevant to your website.

Duplicate these action steps for each article written until all of the desired pages have been added and published.

5.) Disable Comments On Desired Pages or Posts

Locate the page or post that you wish to not display comments on and hover over it to reveal **Quick Edit**. Uncheck **Allow Comments** and click **Update**.

Section 10
WordPress Themes

The Ease of Changing Your Site's Look

Now, it may seem like something is missing when looking at your site. You may think it's

quite boring and that nothing has really changed even though you added all of those

plugins and articles, but the key is starting with the content and then designing the

content to make it visually appealing and extending its functionality.

WordPress allows you to change the look and presentation of the material on your site

by simply installing themes. This feature saves countless hours of coding new CSS and

revamping the HTML. You can simply change the entire design of your website in

minutes with just a few clicks of the mouse and no programming experience is needed.

Free Themes Within WordPress

To change the WordPress theme, click **Themes** in the **Appearance** dropdown menu located in the admin panel. Next, click the **Add New** button at the top of the page.

To browse the large database of themes and bypass the advanced search default, click **Find Themes** at the bottom of the page.

You will now be able to manually search and install themes within this large database just as you would a plugin. These themes are all free, but they may have limited functionality.

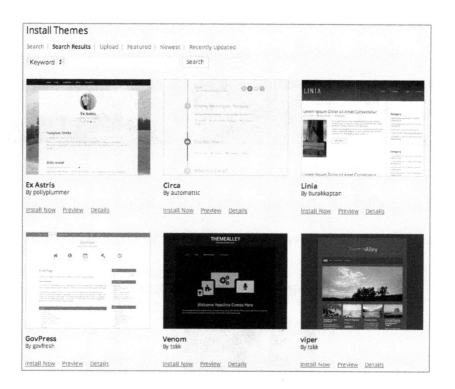

You may ask, "Why are these themes free? What do developers get out of making free themes?" Well, the reason that they are free is because developers are trying to boost their rankings on search engines to acquire free traffic. Search engines use popularity and relevance to determine a website's position in their rankings.

So when a developer creates a new website, he or she builds back links to their newly created site in order to get authority from search engines. The more back links (links from other sites) a website has, the higher it goes up in rankings and therefore, it acquires free traffic.

Shown below, is an example of a free theme and the link

back to the developer's website.

© All rights reserved.
Powered by WordPress & Viper Theme

If a free theme will suffice for your website and you've found one that suits your needs, install it by clicking the **Install Now** link directly below the desired theme.

NewTek
By gamerpotion

Install Now   Preview   Details

Upon clicking **Install Now** WordPress will download, unpack, and install the theme onto your site leaving you with the option to preview or activate it.

Click **Activate** and you will be redirected to the themes menu and the new theme will be present on your site.

Installing Theme: NewTek 1.5.9

Akismet is almost ready. You must enter your Akismet API key for it to work.

Downloading install package from https://wordpress.org/themes/download/newtek.1.5.9.zip...

Unpacking the package...

Installing the theme...

Successfully installed the theme **NewTek 1.5.9.**

Live Preview || Activate || Return to Theme Installer

Familiarize yourself with the theme's features by playing with the settings in the

Appearance menu so you know its capabilities and can manage it with ease.

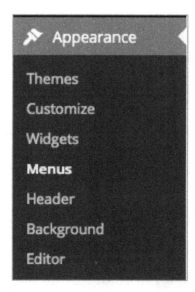

Premium Themes

You can purchase a premium theme if you are not satisfied with any of the free themes available through WordPress. There are several websites that offer them at various price ranges. Premium themes are unique and offer advanced features and functionality. If you run into a problem or need help, customer support is available.

It is not recommended to search for free themes in the search engines even if you can't find anything that suits you. Although there are thousands of them available, they can be very unpredictable and unreliable. By using free themes, you run the risk of downloading malicious code or struggling with the functionality of a poorly written theme and when something goes wrong, there is no customer support.

Your website could potentially be left open to a security breach and your data compromised when a poorly coded theme is used, and now that free theme isn't so free anymore. This can be a costly situation, which you will pay for with time and money.

Although it is not recommended, if you do use a free theme found through your search engine, it is important to download them from reliable sources and the code should be inspected carefully to verify there is no encrypted coding.

Searching For Premium Themes

ThemeForest is a great site to search for premium themes. Their site has a variety of categories that allows users to search themes relevant to a product or service.

To be directed to their site type http://themeforest.net/category/wordpress into the address bar. Use the sidebar to the right to browse available themes.

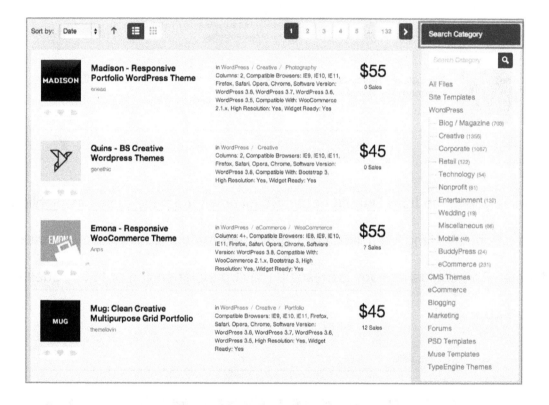

Clicking the title of a desired theme takes you to a page that explains it in greater depth.

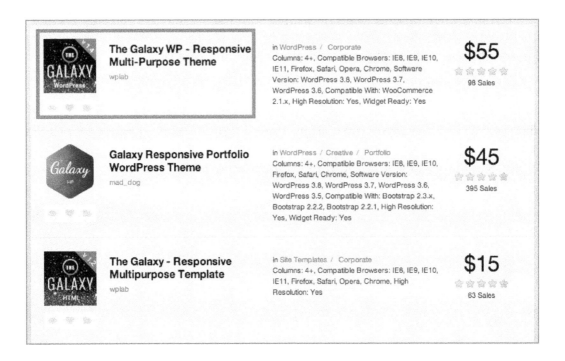

This directs you to the **Item Details** page. Scroll down the page to see its highlighted features before checking it out live. The **Comments** tab contains customer reviews on this theme. To troubleshoot any issues you may be experiencing or to ask questions, click the **Support** tab.

If these features suit your needs, do a live preview and test the site so you know what to expect and can determine if the site's structure and layout meet the needs of your product or service. This allows you to see how the selected theme would look once it is installed on your WordPress. To do this, simply click the **Live Preview** button.

Click on every link, page, post, and drop down menu to see how its navigation works and how all of the plugins and variables are displayed.

Once you have decided which theme to purchase, click **Buy Item** at the top right of the screen.

This will take you back to the theme's description page. You must have an account and be signed in to make a purchase; so if you don't already have an account, you will need to create one. To do this click the **sign up** link. If this isn't your first premium theme purchase and you have an existing account, you can select **sign in**.

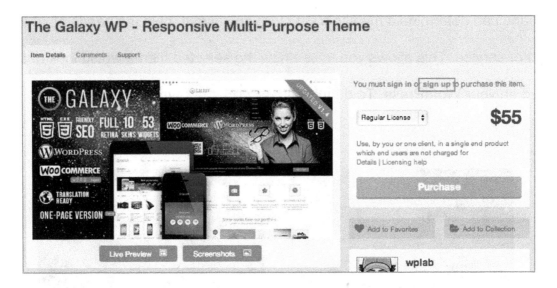

If you are creating an account, you will be prompted to provide information in the necessary fields and click **Create Account**.

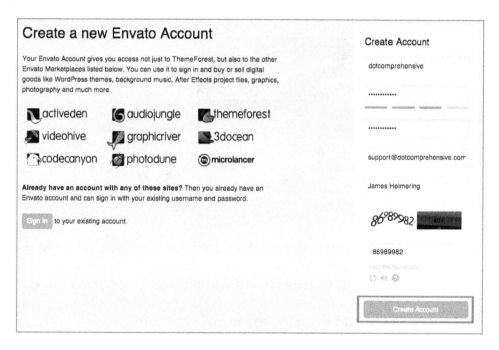

Once the form has been successfully filled out and submitted, you will need to verify your email address to activate the account.

We've sent you an email. Complete the process of creating your account by clicking the link in that email. Bon voyage!

When the account has been successfully activated, return to the theme's detail page and click **Purchase**.

Selecting **Buy Now with PayPal** is the quickest form for acquiring a theme. However,

you may choose to **Add Credit to Buy Now** if you plan on purchasing more themes in

the future and would like to add extra money to your account.

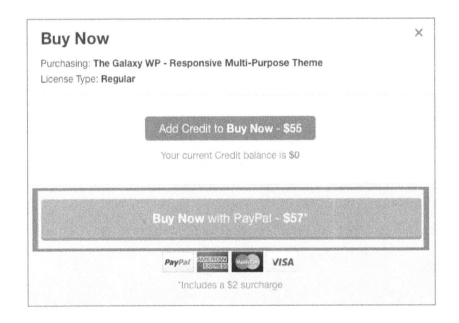

Once your purchase is complete, you can locate your theme by hovering over your username and selecting **Downloads** from the menu.

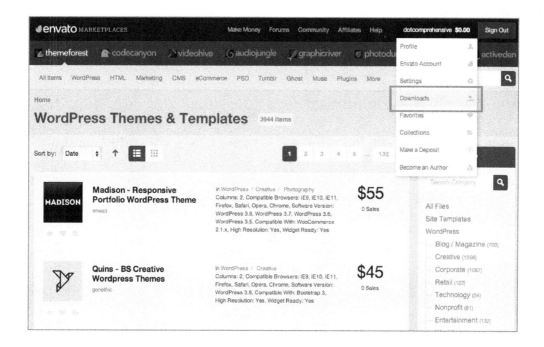

Next, click the **Download** button to the right of your theme. Remember the location of this download because you will need it for installing a new theme on your WordPress.

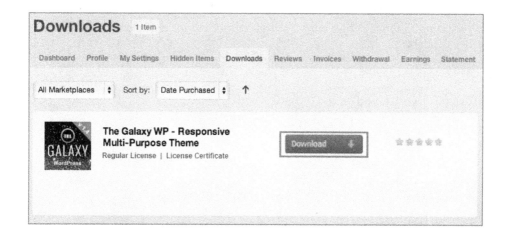

The file should be in a .zip format. A zip file is a file that is compressed for maximum storage or quick transfers via the web. In order for WordPress to allow the theme to be installed, it must stay in this format.

My Theme Wasn't in a .zip Format

If your theme was not in a .zip format, it can be very easily converted into one. The process is very similar between Mac and Pcs. Right click and select **Compress "Galaxy"** for Mac or **Add to Archive** for PC.

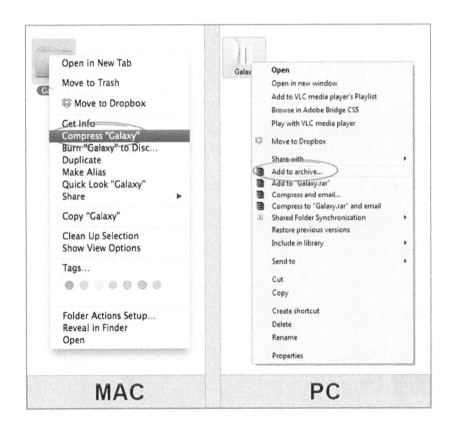

Your operating system will automatically compress the theme and a compressed file will appear next to the original file with a different appearance as shown below.

Galaxy.zip

Galaxy.zip

If the download contained a file similar to this, you are ready to upload it to your WordPress.

Installing Premium Themes

Login to the admin panel within your site by typing yourdomain.com/wp-admin into your browser's address bar or by clicking the **Login** link located under the category labeled **META**. Enter your username and password, if you are not already logged in.

Next, go to your themes menu, which is located on the left hand side. Again, click **Add New**.

Now it's time to upload your newly purchased theme. To do this, click the **Upload** link located at the top of the screen.

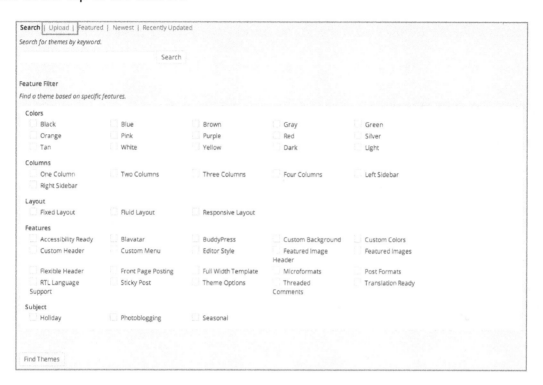

Within this menu, click the button labeled **Choose File** and locate the theme on your computer. Then click **Install Now** to upload it to your site. Remember, it must be in a .zip format.

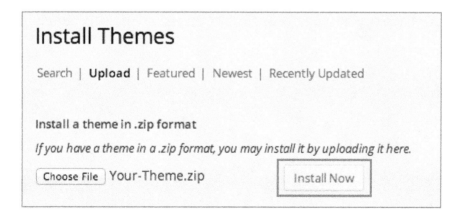

Before the theme becomes active, you will be presented with a preview of what your site will look like with the theme installed. You will have the option to activate it or cancel the action if you aren't happy with the layout or appearance. But keep in mind: your theme hasn't been set up yet so it may not look quite like you had anticipated. You need to go within the themes settings and modify various features and upload images in desired areas to make it look more like the one that was purchased.

If you need help with the settings or have questions, you shouldn't have any problem getting support from the developer. Often times, the developer has a support page and forum for people experiencing difficulty. Try taking a look at their support page, even if you're experienced, because sometimes there might be something to learn.

Activate your theme and feel free to play around with the settings and features.

By going to your website with the new theme installed, you will notice the site looks totally different. Don't worry about how basic it is; this is a work in progress.

Action Step

1.) Change Your WordPress Site's Theme

Determine your budget and decide on a free theme within WordPress or purchase a premium theme with advanced features.

A.) Free Themes Within WordPress

Browse through the free WordPress theme directory and install/activate a theme.

B.) Purchase a Premium Theme

Go to http://themeforest.net/category/wordpress and purchase a premium theme. Download the theme to your computer and upload it to your themes menu within the WordPress admin panel.

To upload the theme, locate the downloaded file (in .zip format) after clicking the **Add New** button. Once the download has been located, install the theme and activate it.

Section 11
Testing

Testing Your Site

It is very important to test your site and its capabilities. Otherwise, you may not know if your site is functioning properly.

Before sharing your site with the world, test it by using the top three browsers that searchers might potentially use. Since people use different browsers, a website's features or preferences may vary in look and/or functionality.

At the beginning of this book, you downloaded and installed Safari, Internet Explorer, Firefox, and Google Chrome. Each of these browsers may present your site in a different manner and <u>MAY</u> cause it to look differently or function incorrectly.

Each time you make a change to the look of your site, update, add a plugin, or affix a new feature it should be tested on every browser. If something isn't functioning properly, you can evaluate the problem and make the necessary changes to fix it.

If you are having difficulties finding the issue, try taking a look at the developer's forum or blog and you may find something to help resolve the problem. If you are using a free theme and cannot find developer support, search Google for a solution.

Action Step

1.) Test Your Site on Multiple Browsers

Before continuing, open each browser that you installed at Introduction of this book.

Browsers to Test Your Site

Internet Explorer

Safari - apple.com/safari

Firefox - http://firefox.com

Google Chrome - http://google.com/chrome

Internet Explorer is not available to Mac users. If you are using a PC, you already have

Internet Explorer installed by default.

Section 12
Backlinks

Building Backlinks

By now, your site should be up and running. However, without visitors, it is a pointless piece of real estate on the Internet. There are two general methods for receiving site traffic outside of social networking: paid traffic (*PPC*) and organic traffic via *SEO*.

If you don't have a lot of money to spend on advertisements, then your best option is to receive traffic organically, meaning through the search engines. In order to do this, your site must have high quality, unique, relevant content as well as links from other sites that point to your site and its pages. These are called backlinks.

What is a Backlink?

A backlink is an incoming hyperlink from one web page to another website. The more backlinks you have pointing back to your site, the more popular it will be (*google.com 2014*).

Ways to Build Quality Backlinks

Building backlinks is not a cakewalk. It takes a lot of man-hours to create quality backlinks from authoritative sites. It is also wise to ensure the majority of sites that link to you contain content relevant to your site. There are several ways to build backlinks to a site, some of which include:

1.) Asking / Exchanging Links

Often you can find the site owner's email address or contact page and ask if they would add a link to your site from theirs. If they do not wish to add your link, you could offer to exchange links with them. Meaning you will add a link to their site onto your site, and they return the kind gesture.

2.) Paying For Links

You probably don't want to spend any money if not required to, but sometimes giving a site/company with high authority several bucks for a link may actually pay off.

There are also other forms of payment for backlinks that you can negotiate, such as offering a particular skill. Example, if you majored in literature and find grammar/punctuation errors on their site, there is your selling point. *I majored in literature and I see quite a few grammar, spelling, and punctuation errors within your site. If you will place a link back to my site, I will edit 3 of your site's pages.*

3.) Provide Content Value

You learned a great method of writing quick quality material in this book, now you can put it to use. There are several areas on the web that will allow a link back to your site for quality content.

Forums will often allow you to put a signature back to your site after so many posts. However, make sure you read their rules and actually provide value in the forum. Don't just post randomly until you are allowed to add your signature. Most forums will terminate you for this. ***Number One Forum Rule:*** Do the research, provide value to others within forums, and earn the respect and trust of the community before you start linking back to your site within a signature. Trust me, they will see right through your actions if you don't abide by that rule.

4.) Hire a SEO Company

Again, spending money is risky, but risks often turn into rewards. I have had a lot of luck in the past hiring SEO companies to build links to my sites. I have also had a lot of bad experiences before I knew what I was doing. I thought hiring a cheap company was okay. I figured there is no wrong way to build links. Sadly, I was wrong. My sites soared to the top in a couple months, then plummeted off the face of the search engines.

Cheaper companies often use automated software that basically spams sites with a link to yours. Sure you will rank high for a few days, maybe even a few months. But soon the search engines will see right through these actions and drop you off the face of the earth.

Article Marketing

Article Marketing is another way of providing valuable content in exchange for a link. There are oodles of article marketing sites out there, and plenty of subjects to write about which means more potential links to your site.

With article marketing you must make sure to read their terms of use. Understand this, although article marketing directories are one of the easiest ways to build backlinks, they will not tolerate any spamming behavior either. Just like with forums: do your research, understand your topic, and add the link back to your site (or page you wish to generate more traffic to).

Article marketing directories are a bit more lenient than forums; they actually insist you post a link back to your site. But do not try to abuse this privilege by attempting to add 100 links within your article because it will not work.

Eventually, you will likely use all of these link-building techniques. Though, you should get started right away with the free methods such as forum posts and writing articles for article directories.

Before you sign up to any forum, determine the type of product or service you offer. Next, search for forums related to your topic by typing the subject in the search engine's search bar, e.g., website building forums.

Article directories allow you to create unlimited articles within your account. Sign up to each of the following article marketing directories and write your heart out ensuring each article relates to the site that needs a backlink.

List of Article Directories

Courtesy of http://www.vretoolbar.com/

ehow.com examiner.com hubpages.com squidoo.com ezinearticles.com

seekingalpha.com technorati.com apsense.com/article/start

goarticles.comarticlesbase.com buzzle.com textbroker.com biggerpockets.com/articles

amazines.com sooperarticles.com knoji.com/articles/ triond.com brighthub.com

articletrader.com thefreelibrary.com articlesnatch.com gather.com suite101.com

isnare.com articlecity.com infobarrel.com ezinemark.com articlerich.com artipot.com

pubarticles.com EvanCarmichael.com articlealley.com articlesfactory.com

articlecube.com articledashboard.com thewhir.com/find/articlecentral streetarticles.com

upublish.info informationbible.com abcarticledirectory.com articles.org articlebro.com

xgbook.com submityourarticle.com/articles/ articledirectoryusa.com earticlesonline.com

articlecell.com articlestars.com constant-content.com

This book does not go into great detail on search engine optimization due to the constant algorithm changes. Please educate yourself on SEO and stay up-to-date with the latest algorithm changes to ensure your site maintains its ranking.

Action Steps

1.) Build Links Back to Your Site

A.) Ask / Exchange for Links

Email websites and kindly ask them to place a link on their page to your site. Sweeten the pot by agreeing to do a link exchange.

B.) Pay For Links

Email websites and offer money or a service/skill in exchange for a link back to your site.

C.) Provide Valuable Content

Forum Content

Determine your product or service and find related forums. Read the terms of use and rules provided on each forum before making any posts. Provide value to the forum and NEVER spam. When the option becomes available, edit your signature in order to receive a link back to your site.

D.) Hire a SEO Company

Hire a company that specializes in search engine optimization. Do your homework on each company you interview before hiring. Check customer feedback, amount of work, and don't be afraid to ask them about their link building techniques. The only secret for building links is hard work, or going viral. If they can't discuss their methods with you, don't hire them. Also remember, you get what you pay for.

Write For Article Directories

Determine your product or service and write related articles. Sign up to the list of article directories listed in this section and read the terms of use and rules provided on each directory before making any posts. Provide value to the article directory and NEVER spam.

Section 13
Customer Service

Providing Excellence

Customer service is one of the most important aspects of running any type of business.

It can change a customer's entire outlook on a company's product or service. Poor

customer service could harm your company even if you have a great product, whereas

great customer service could actually improve sales of a crummy product or service.

Maintaining customer satisfaction is especially important when running an online

business. The quality of service provided will greatly depend on the success of your

business. It also plays a major role in increasing revenue and maintaining your

company's stability.

There is always room for improvement when dealing with customer service, in conjunction with product tweaks. Improvements will not only keep existing customers happy, but it will also bring in new customers, meaning an increase in profit. That's why so many businesses today consistently test and adjust their service because, they know, quality equals value and value equals an increase in revenue.

Adapting to Your Customers

Being able to adjust your personality to a customer's temperament or having a very diverse staff is an important skill. It may be difficult for some to acquire this, but it can be learned with experience resulting in more sales.

Creating a virtual one-on-one connection is more difficult to accomplish than it would be to connect person-to-person. That is why it is imperative to obtain an understanding of the customer's needs and expectations while relating to him or her personally to appropriately address their issue to the fullest of your capabilities.

Go Above and Beyond

Exceeding the expectations of your customers will astound them and also give them something to talk about to their friends. In 2010 I ran a company called Beadiful Rosaries. It was a site that allowed people to build a custom rosary or bracelet by selecting particular beads, colors, and links.

These rosaries were built, packaged, and mailed by me. I also served as the only customer service rep. Often customers called the 800 line wanting things that I did not offer. My plate was usually already full, but I still went the extra mile when possible.

One example is when a man called about getting two rosaries made for his parents' 50th anniversary. He wanted each rosary individually wrapped along with a personal message and to be delivered within 2 days although the turnaround for building a custom rosary was 2 weeks. We did not offer any of these services, but I accepted this challenge and stayed up all night crafting two one-of-a-kind rosaries. Not only did I wrap both rosaries in special boxes, I also went out of my way to purchase an appropriate 50th anniversary card and included the son's personal message to his parents within, hand-written.

Even though the only shipping method was 3-5 days, I spent the money to expedite the shipping to ensure the gifts arrived on his parent's doorstep the next day at no extra charge.

Weeks later, I received an email from the son stating Beadiful Rosaries had the best customer service he had ever experienced before in his life. He thanked us for all of the extra work we did and days later we received orders from 3 others recommended by him.

This is a perfect example of how you can go beyond the expectations of your customers to generate more revenue for your company. So take my advice, take care of your customers and they will take care of you.

Know What You're Selling

It's your product; you should know it inside and out, even if you didn't actually create it yourself. Study it, understand it, always have an answer for everything, and be ready for anything.

Often, your customers may stump you with a question. It has happened to me many times although I knew my product like the back of my hand. If a customer leaves you baffled with a question, take a minute to find out the answer.

If you're on the phone with a customer, get a call back number and call them as soon as you discover the answer. Time is more on your side if a mind-boggling email is received but you still need to promptly ruminate/research and address the question.

Like I said, I have been stumped many times and so will you. It's not terrible that you don't have an answer for everything, but it's bad business to leave someone puzzled and harmful to the overall customer experience of your company to have an unrequited answer.

Your Customers Build The Product

You came up with an idea by solving a problem, created the product, and gave it a home. But your product is only as good as your customers perceive it to be. As your company grows, so must the products within it. It's going to take time to refine your business but the good news is you won't have to do it alone. With Beadiful Rosaries my customers were providing me with enough feedback, good and bad, that kept me unceasingly busy.

Part of providing great customer service means making changes where necessary based off of issues that have been discovered by you and your customers. Change is good and taking action toward bettering the overall use of your website, product or service, and customer service will help stimulate the growth of your business resulting in an increase of revenue.

Companies that possess teams of employees dedicated to improving the overall success of a company still does not compare to the vast majority of people who pay the company's bills (customers).

When you create a product, no matter how wonderful it is, long before it is complete. You will need to constantly evolve your product in order to meet your customer's demands. If your product can't consistently gratify their needs, they will find something that can.

Always be prepared to amend your product. Sometimes changes may be as small as a spelling error. Other times it could be a large update. But don't feel like you've failed if a total transformation is required. Evolution is a necessity for all businesses in order to sustain its current customers, establish new ones, and continue growing.

Obtaining Your Customer's Opinion

So how do you know what your customer thinks? How they feel? What they would like to see in the future? Thanks to technology, it's very easy.

One of the quickest ways of obtaining your customer's opinion is by adding a forum/blog on your site where customers can communicate to other customers and share their experience or receive troubleshooting guides.

These types of communication ports allow you, as a company, to examine very specific and often detailed information that can be incorporated into your product or service's next update. The information in these portals is very valuable. Not only will it help the improvement of your company, it may also take off a portion of the workload as the venue warrants people helping people.

Asking for your customer's opinion is another way of obtaining feedback but the repetitiveness of this method may take valuable time, especially if you are communicating through email. Also, most customers are not as specific through email as they are through a community support page.

Don't dismiss this technique of ascertaining feedback; instead, improvise through automation. There are systems available online that automatically send out surveys to existing customers which can help determine a customer's thoughts without wasting too much of anybody's time. But these automated systems have rules.

Your customers have lives too. So, do yourself a favor and don't overwhelm them with hundreds of questions. Get to the point and ask questions that will help you improve your product's overall capabilities. If you are reluctant to do so, the customer will simply close out of the survey because long, boring forms are a waste of time.

Live Chat Sessions

One of the things you installed on your website is the Zopim chat widget. The reason I had you install this is because it's a great form of instantly communicating with your customers.

Being able to start a conversation with someone as soon as they reach your storefront grants you the ability to guide them in the right direction. Communication will essentially form a relationship between you and the shopper, ultimately creating a comfortable shopping experience with the probability of a sale.

Customer Phone Support

With the luxuries of the Internet, phone support is not as crucial as it was in stone ages of business. However, sometimes it can be beneficial because people like conversing verbally rather than sending an email and waiting for a reply.

When I managed Beadiful Rosaries, communicating over the phone was my customer's first and last choice for conversing. The only customer emails received were responses to pictures I sent out of their completed rosary for approval or when kindly requesting a testimonial for the site.

Nonetheless, phone support may or may not benefit your company as it did mine, but it doesn't hurt it either. I would suggest for those who plan on selling physical products to consider a phone line. But if the product being sold is digital, contemplate the perplexity of it to determine the need of a support line.

For instance, a digital book is pretty straightforward. It's unlikely that any confusion will arise from reading a sales page to navigating to the checkout page, unless of course your site is at fault. If that is the case, maybe you should consider giving your site a face-life with easier navigation.

Having phone support for a digital product relating to software or online service is controversial. This comes down to the complexity of your software or service and how well the documentation of the product is explained. If you feel that your product is in need of an 800 number, I recommend Grasshopper.

Acquiring a Grasshopper account will allow you to run your business anywhere, anytime. This service was developed for diligent entrepreneurs who are always on the go. With Grasshopper you can run your business using a cell phone, meaning you don't have to physically be at the office to provide customer support.

Born online, Grasshopper offers a variety of services starting at $12.00 a month with a rate of about $.06 cents a minute. Choose a number, record your greeting, add departments, and start accepting phone calls wherever you may be.

Having this service puts a nice touch on a business that demands one-on-one support with its customers and associates, and adds a higher level of professionalism to your customer service.

Regardless of the various support options you provide to your customers, the most important role for you, as well as your company, is to ensure that the customer's satisfaction is maintained and will continue to grow with your business along with the never-ending changes in technology. In conclusion, remember that with customer service, there is always room for improvement and something new to learn.

Closure
The Indefinite Conclusion

This book is just the beginning of an enduring adventure that you must take. As technology continues to evolve, so must your skills and education.

Never stop halfway through your journey to a successful website; turning around is often more challenging than continuing forward and reaching the finish line.

The tools provided here were designed to guide you in the right direction. The choice to use what you have learned and fulfill your goals is an obvious justification.

I give you my best wishes.

To successful site creation…

Good Luck!

James Helmering

Resources

"Domain names" *Wikipedia: The Free Encyclopedia.* Wikimedia Foundation, Inc., date

last updated (22 March 2014). Web. Date accessed (29 March 2014).

http://en.wikipedia.org/wiki/Domain_name.

"Backlinks" Google: *Search the world's information, including webpages, images, videos

and more.* Google Public Data, Inc.; Web. Date accessed (29 March 2014).

https://www.google.com/#q=Define+backlinks

Trademark Notification

Any **(or all)** uses of screenshots in this material that contain evidence of trademark entities are used solely for educational purposes and are **NOT** intended to diminish the name or quality of products produced by the providing establishment.

These images are believed to be of low-resolution and may qualify as **fair use** under the United States copyright law.

The supplier of this material agrees to comply with any submissions from parties (*possessing ownership*) who feel the images are copyright infringement and will remove, edit, or take other necessary actions to ensure demands are met.

To make any report regarding infringement contact the .comPREHENSIVE legal department via email legal@dotcomprehensive.com and state your concerns.

© .comPREHENSIVE 2014 All Rights Reserved

www.ingramcontent.com/pod-product-compliance
Lightning Source LLC
Chambersburg PA
CBHW080413060326
40689CB00019B/4228